**DO NOT REMOVE
CARDS FROM POCKET**

Radio
Hole-in-the-Head

Radio Liberty

Radio
Hole-in-the-Head

Radio Liberty

An Insider's Story of Cold War Broadcasting

James Critchlow

The American University Press
Washington, DC

Copyright © 1995 by
The American University Press
4400 Massachusetts Avenue, NW
Washington, DC 20016

Distributed by arrangement with
University Publishing Associates
4720 Boston Way
Lanham, Maryland 20706

3 Henrietta Street
London, WC2E 8LU England

Library of Congress Cataloging-in-Publication Data

Critchlow, James.
Radio hole-in-the-head/Radio Liberty : an insider's story of Cold War
broadcasting / James Critchlow
p. cm.
1. Radio Liberty (Munich, Germany)—History. 2. RFE/RL, inc.—
History. 3. International broadcasting. 4. Radio in propaganda—
United States—History. 5. Cold War. I. Title.
HE8697.4.C75   1995   95-32855   384.54'06'543364—dc20   CIP

ISBN 1-879383-47-0 (cloth: alk: ppr.)
ISBN 1-879383-48-9 (pbk: alk: ppr.)

To those lively souls of many nationalities who came together, against odds, to form the improbable team that turned "Radio Hole-in-the-Head" into Radio Liberty

Contents

Photographs follow page 96

Acknowledgements

My thanks to those who helped by providing photographs for the illustrations, expecially Joan Balcar; Gerda Pylajew-Pawlowsky; Francis Ronalds; Jon Sawyer; Anatole Shub; Tanja Venzl; Solveig Baldauf, Kevin Klose and Jane Lester of RFE/RL, Inc. Richard T. Davies encouraged me at various stages of the writing and editorial process. Francis and Adair Ronalds read portions of the text and made helpful suggestions, as did McKinney and Lydie Russell. Richard Rowson and David Burke of The American University Press have been of great assistance throughout. Responsibility for the final content is solely my own.

Author's Note

Some of the dialogue reported in this book appears in quotation marks as direct quotations. People have asked me how it is possible, so many years after the events, to remember what was said verbatim. The answer: my use of quotations is limited to conversations that were unusually striking at the time, the kind of thing that you review over and over in your own mind and in reliving the past with others. In those cases I am certain that a written transcript, if there were one, would differ only in minor respects from what I have written.

Prologue

The end of the Cold War has turned the world upside down in more ways than one.

In March 1993 Mikhail Gorbachev attended a reception held in Moscow to honor Radio Liberty's fortieth anniversary, and said he now listens regularly to Radio Liberty broadcasts. He was talking about the station that is credited today as a major catalyst in the political softening that led to collapse of the Soviet Union he headed.

One of the other guests at the Moscow party for Radio Liberty was a KGB general. Such people were once at the pinnacle of a system that resorted to extraordinary measures, even murder, to try to destroy us at Radio Liberty in Munich.

In the earliest Munich days we at Radio Liberty had other enemies, too. Senator Joe McCarthy and his followers were looking for victims who could be branded "red" or "pink." It made no difference that the real Reds in the Kremlin were out to do us in.

Then there were those kibitzers who merely poked fun at our nondescript gang of unruly American intellectuals and threadbare refugees from the Soviet Union. They mocked us for abandoning political and bureaucratic orthodoxy to cobble together our offbeat station. They were the ones who called us "Radio Hole-in-the-Head."

Against all expectations we managed—beginning with our first feeble broadcasts in 1953—to lay the foundation of an effective communication instrument with a personality of its own and an audience of millions inside the Soviet Union. We thought up program ideas that shaped the broadcasts for decades to come. And together with our band of Russians, Ukrainians, Tatars, Uzbeks, Armenians, Azerbaijanis—not to mention Balkars, Chechens, Karakalpaks, and others even more exotic to Americans—we experienced years of difficulties and occasional dangers, of frustration mixed with fun.

Our job was to create an American-funded radio that would address its listeners in the Soviet Union in the name of the former Soviet citizens, now in the West, who would be our broadcasters. Each nationality would have its own language service. Russians would speak to Russians, or Tatars to Tatars, in terms of their common historical experience and shared cultural values. (At one point, there were more than twenty language services.) Programs would focus on events in the homeland that were suppressed or distorted by the censored official media. It was reasoned that a radio of that kind would evoke a special response from its audiences. In this respect it would be different from the governmental Voice of America: although the Voice also broadcast in Russian and some of our other languages, its basic mission could be summed up in the slogan "telling America's story to the world," making it to listeners a foreign medium, however great the popularity of some of its broadcasts (especially its programs of American jazz).

Back in Washington, D.C., there was another consideration in the conception of our radio. It would be easier for the U.S. government to disclaim responsibility for the broadcasts of a "private" radio in case the Kremlin complained about them. The fiction of Radio Liberty's nongovernmental sponsorship fooled hardly anyone, certainly not the Soviet government, but it helped the State Department and its diplomatic staff to relax. To us in Munich, whether our radio was public or private made little difference, as long as the broadcasts could speak for themselves, without official censorship.

The model that our sponsors had in mind was Radio Free Europe, whose programs beamed to Poland, Czechoslovakia, and other Soviet "satellite" countries were already on the air when Radio Liberty was conceived. But we soon found that the specifics of broadcasting to Soviet audiences, and the kind of people available to do it, created a whole new set of problems. This book tells how we rose to that challenge.

Did Radio Liberty do its job well? It gained millions of daily listeners, despite the insistent grinding noise of hundreds of Soviet jamming stations trying to blot it out. Some of its listeners even managed to tape the broadcasts and stealthily circulate transcripts to their friends. Soviet propaganda officials conducted an elaborately orchestrated campaign, through the controlled mass media and oral "agitation" lectures, to discredit the station and those of us who worked for it. After the Soviet Union collapsed, there was a chorus of praise from people in its audience. But much remains to be learned about the extent to which the broadcasts actually influenced the political process—a task for future generations of researchers.

Ironically, Radio Liberty is little known in the United States, the country that created it and paid its bills for more than forty years. For the most part, the station has not been good media copy. Americans are more apt to know Radio Liberty from its fictional portrayal in Martin Cruz Smith's best-selling thriller *Red Square* than from any more coherent source. Yet the true story of RL is full of fascination.

I missed the Moscow meeting, but I have tasted Radio Liberty's new post–Cold War prestige during other visits deep inside former Soviet territory. On one occasion, the government of newly sovereign Kazakstan asked Radio Liberty's research office (a department that I once headed) to set up a conference on problems of independence. Kazakstan is the ninth largest nation in the world by size—a land-locked, beautiful country that borders China. I was asked to come from Harvard University to give a paper on democratization. Later, it amused me to learn that none of the Radio Liberty officials who invited me knew I had been an early employee of their organization, that I was one of the handful of young Americans with college Russian who in 1952 had gone to Munich to create the new radio station.

Kazakstan's tree-lined capital city of Almaty is a pleasant place with spectacular views of the towering snowcapped peaks of the Trans-Ili range of the Tien Shan mountains. Sitting under television lights in a spacious government building, I listened to speaker after speaker praising Radio Liberty. How many of those Kazak officials, I wondered, had once made speeches condemning us at Radio Liberty as a "mouthpiece of imperialism"?

Waiting for my own turn to speak, I began to reminisce about Radio Liberty's birth pains.

It all began with Stalin's death.

Stalin Dies, We Live

1

In the darkness of the Munich hotel room, I reached for the ringing telephone. It was Boris, his voice vibrant with excitement.

"He's dying. Wake up and turn on Moscow."

I fought sleep and looked at my watch. It was 5 A.M.

"Who's dying?"

"*He* is. Stalin. The old boy. Get your radio on and tell your wife I'm coming down for breakfast." Boris Shub and his wife Libby lived two floors above us. Unlike her restless husband, she was not a morning person.

Waiting for the vacuum tubes of the German shortwave radio to warm up, I managed to mutter to Pat the two news items, about Stalin and her breakfast guest. She switched on the hot plate and began to bring in groceries from the window ledge, our makeshift refrigerator. It was typical of our awe of Boris Shub's genius that she did not protest his claim on her hospitality at this uncivil hour.

Radio Moscow came on in mid-sentence. It was a medical bulletin, the announcer's deep male voice theatrically slow and solemn. That was either Levitan, whose dramatic reading of victory communiqués during the war had made him famous to Soviet listeners, or someone who sounded like him. A few sentences later, the treatment being given Stalin was described. Incredibly, the bulletin mentioned the use of leeches to bleed him.

For anyone on that day of March 4, 1953, the serious illness of the seemingly invincible tyrant who had enslaved half of Europe and much of Asia, who headed a powerful international political movement, who had nuclear armies poised to strike at many parts of the world, was a momentous event. For those of us in Munich who had succeeded only a few days earlier, on March 1, in putting a new radio station on the air to broadcast to the peoples of the Soviet Union, it was a special challenge, one for which we were ill prepared.

Riding out to the station on the Munich outskirts after devouring Pat's bacon and eggs, Shub outlined to me his ideas for coping with the crisis. Boris was the policy advisor to our fledgling radio station, sent over temporarily from New York headquarters to help get us on the air.

We would have to scrap our broadcast reserve, he insisted, the programs that we had been laboriously taping for weeks. History was now upon us. Breaking news and world comment would be the priority, with documentaries to put Stalin's career into accurate perspective. "Without a lot of anti-Commie crap," Shub told me. "And no emotion, no garbage," he added, "there'll be plenty of that from Moscow. And no gloating, no *Schadenfreude*. Remember, as far as we know, millions of people worship the old bastard."

The warning against "anti-Commie crap" had more than a little point in those Cold War days. Six weeks before our Radio Liberation (RL, later renamed Radio Liberty) went on the air, on January 15, 1953, president-elect Dwight Eisenhower's secretary of state–designate John Foster Dulles had appealed before a Senate committee for "liberation" of the "captive peoples." Dulles qualified his appeal by saying that "liberation does not mean a war of liberation," but many of his followers ignored the qualification. We were under constant pressure, from both Americans and émigrés from the Soviet bloc, to make our radio into the tactical spearhead of a Western military force advancing into the Communist world.

The setting for all this was postwar Munich, much of it still in ruins from the Allied bombings. At the end of a hall on each floor of the Regina-Palast Hotel, where most of the American staff of RL were housed, a door was kept tightly locked: to step through it meant dropping into a bomb crater below. From the street, pedestrians could look up to the fourth floor and see a bathtub still hanging from the wall by its pipes.

In Munich there were constant reminders of war and Nazi rule. We sometimes ate in the American officers' club in the Haus der Deutschen Kunst, a mammoth columned building that Hitler had turned into a shrine of "nondecadent," purely Aryan German art. Down the street was a house where the Führer himself had lived. One of the best restaurants in town was the Osteria Italiana on Schellingstrasse, which had been Hitler's favorite and where the waitresses told stories of his visits. Restaurant menus still listed *Echtbohnenkaffee* (real bean coffee) to reassure you that you were not being served the spurious *Ersatzkaffee* of the Hitler and early postwar years.

There were other signs of the demoralizing effects of the Nazi period and its aftermath. On Möhlstrasse in the Bogenhausen district, respectable Bavarian *Bürger* would rub shoulders with Americans and other *Zugeroaste* (dialect for immigrants) at a flourishing black market. Here one could buy cigarettes and coffee supplied from their rations, in violation of regulations, by American military personnel and their spouses. Otherwise virtuous women would trade sex for a good job or a few cartons of cigarettes. Pervading the atmosphere were the petty spitefulness and selfishness toward one another of people seared by the wartime struggle for survival, a side that they seldom displayed to us conquering Americans. For our part, flush with our dollar wealth (enhanced in many cases by black market transactions) and basking in the euphoria of victory, we were all too ready to let people raise us to the pedestal of supermen.

As the principal city in the American Zone of military occupation, Munich had attracted a large concentration of refugees from the East: Germans, Poles, Czechs, Russians, Ukrainians, anyone whose homeland had come under Communist rule. They had been resettled in the barracks of the DP (displaced person) camps that ringed the city. Some of the men were organized by the U.S. Army into paramilitary national labor units and wore uniforms; I remember seeing one individual with "Albanian" on his shoulder patch. By 1952, when Pat and I arrived in Munich, many of the DPs had found regular jobs or emigrated to North America and Australia, but thousands still lived in the camps. With the Cold War at its height, the camps and the desperate unemployed who inhabited them were a magnet for the recruitment efforts of various intelligence services, both Communist and anti-Communist.

RL's embryonic operation was located in the Oberwiesenfeld district on the outskirts of Munich. The oblong gray building assigned to us there by the American Military Government was a kind of historic landmark, the operations building of the prewar Munich airport. There in 1938 Hitler had greeted the British and French prime ministers when they arrived for the conference that sealed Czechoslovakia's fate. The field from which Oberwiesenfeld took its name was a large open area that offered no protection from winter gales. The building itself, damaged during the war, had its insides hastily rebuilt for our occupancy, and throughout our first winter the gray damp of the Bavarian climate was accentuated by the wet walls of our offices. After we had been there for a few years, the defeated Germans regained the right to have civil aircraft; a local flying club, deprived of our building, operated out of a shack at a distant edge of the field. Some of the members decided to get the building back by scaring us out of it, and for a few days (until the authorities put a stop to it), I would look out the window of my corner office to see a plane headed right for me, piloted by some frustrated ex-Luftwaffe ace who would peel off and just miss the corner at the last second. Many years later, after I had left Munich, the building was razed to make room for the Olympic Center that housed the 1972 summer games; someone sent me a clipping from a local newspaper reporting that six unexploded British high-explosive bombs had been found underneath our old offices. It was at those games that Israeli athletes were murdered, not far from the former site of RL.

During our taxi ride out to Oberwiesenfeld on that chilly March morning in 1953, Boris mused about the announcement that Stalin was being bled with leeches. It intrigued him. "Crazy medieval way to treat a stroke, as I'm sure the doctors know," he commented. "They must think that's what the Soviet masses want to hear." (Years later we learned from Stalin's daughter, Svetlana Alliluyeva, that leeches really were used.)

As we pulled up at our building in Oberwiesenfeld across the street from the *Trummerhaufen,* a small mountain of rubble that was all that remained of much of Munich, Boris turned to me with a wicked grin. "I bet you guys are sorry now I let you talk me out of the metronome."

Weeks before our new radio went on the air, Boris had had a pilot station break taped by a Russian announcer in a New York studio. Over the ticking sound of a metronome, the announcer would repeat rhythmically, "Epokha Stalina podkhodit k kontsu, Epokha Stalina podkhodit k kontsu" (The era of Stalin is coming to the end, the era of Stalin is coming to the end . . .). When Boris had played the tape in Munich for a mixed group of us, Russians and Americans, somebody pointed out that Stalin, then seventy-three, could live to be a hundred. After all, he was a Georgian. We would be out on an embarrassing limb. Reluctantly, Boris conceded. If he had stuck to his guns, on this day of Stalin's stroke RL would have looked like an oracle, achieving instant worldwide fame.

Getting out of the car, Boris sighed ruefully. "You were right, though. It was too big a chance to take."

We were admitted to the building by the guards, black-uniformed Germans employed by a private security firm with the guttural name of Münchner Wach- und Schliessgesellschaft, the Munich Guard and Lock Company. Inside, things were just beginning to wake up. People hurried through long, narrow corridors of the four-story structure to their posts, some pausing to discuss the news in small groups. On the first floor, a knot were clustered around a DPA (Deutsche Presseagentur) ticker, our only wire-service resource, which was spewing out items in German. After a glance, Shub and I headed for the second-floor office of Manning Williams.

With the title of radio advisor, Williams was the top-ranking American in the building. He was a former West Virginia country journalist who had joined the State Department and served in Moscow after World War II. With his straggly, curly hair prematurely white, Williams wore an expression of permanent bemusement, as if he had just awakened. Williams's immediate superior, a shadowy figure named Otis Peabody Swift, preferred to maintain his headquarters in the warmth and comfort of the Regina-Palast Hotel, where most of the rest of us in the American contingent were also quartered. In his office-bedroom suite, Swift kept three electric heaters going and always wore a sweater, while his visitors sweltered. He reported in turn to Admiral Leslie Stevens in New York, head of the militantly named American Committee for Liberation of the Peoples of Russia, our employer. Stevens had once been assigned as naval attaché at the American Embassy in Moscow, had developed feelings of great warmth for the Russian people, and had written a book based on his observations of the scene. The committee had been incorporated in Delaware under the Truman administration.

The group that assembled that morning to discuss radio coverage of Stalin's illness and possible death included Williams, Shub, Edmund Stevens, and—part of the time—Francis Ronalds and myself. Stevens, a Pulitzer Prize–winning former Moscow correspondent on leave from the *Christian Science Monitor,* had been brought to Munich to try to set up a professional news operation. He was a distant cousin of Admiral Stevens, although I never heard him invoke the relationship. "Ronny" Ronalds, after graduation from Princeton and the Russian Institute at Columbia University, had worked four years for *Time* magazine before coming to Munich. During World War II, after receiving Russian-language training in the U.S. Navy, Ronalds was assigned as liaison officer with Soviet naval units in Germany and Austria.

Ronalds and I, both in our mid-twenties, were easily the youngest present. But when management decisions were made, we were the ones assigned to explain them in Russian to the émigré staff and to try to get them implemented through whatever mixture of pleading and cajolery we could muster. The two of us were called assistant radio advisors, but Ronalds was senior to me, having arrived in Munich the previous July, a month before I did. I was very much the baby of the group in terms of political savvy and experience. An engineering graduate, I had spent a year learning Russian in order to get out of my rut at the General Electric Company in Schenectady, New York. I had read just about every Russian classic that I could get my hands on, but my practical experience was limited to writing a few freelance articles on Soviet affairs and earning money by translating works from Russian, one of them a 700-page book on foot-and-mouth disease.

Ronalds and I were accustomed to being banished from Manning Williams's office while he discussed actions that the two of us, as the frontline Americans at RL, would then be called on to implement. We attended only part of the meeting that morning, but we were present long enough to get a good sense of the heated interaction between Shub and Stevens on the one hand, and Williams on the other. Boris filled us in on the rest after it was over.

Despite the excitement of the news from Moscow and the opportunity for change that it promised, Boris told us later that morning, the mood in Williams's office was tinged with gloom: our resources for covering Stalin's death agony were pathetic.

For one thing, RL was hung up in politics. It was conceived as an independent station of refugees from the Soviet Union—or émigrés, as they called themselves—for which the U.S. side would provide only technical facilities and advice. The advice was to be taken or disregarded, at the whim of the émigré chiefs. To provide a political base, various émigré factions—"parties" representing different Soviet nationalities—had been coaxed and wheedled into coming together in a "Co-ordinating Center for Anti-Bolshevik Struggle." This ineptly high-sounding name, with which Soviet propagandists had fun, was the result of exhausting negotiations nudged along by the American representatives. Creation of the center, which had dragged on for months, was feted at a victory banquet at the Bayrischer Hof, one of Munich's most luxurious hotels, which Pat and I attended. There were speeches in some twenty languages. The lengthy proceedings were soured by the exuberant drunkenness of a senior American executive, who became impatient at the speechmaking and began to rip eighteenth-century oil paintings from the walls of our ornate private dining room. Next he flicked drops from his martini into the face of Jehun Bey Hajibeyli, a stately elderly Azerbaijani who had been one of his region's delegates to the Versailles Peace Conference. "I hereby christen thee," he told the shocked old Muslim in broken Russian.

By the time RL went on the air, only three days before news of Stalin's stroke, the Co-ordinating Center had already begun to come unstuck, but some of its leaders clung tenaciously to their prerogatives. On one occasion, an excited employee came rushing breathlessly down from one of the studios on the third floor to summon American help. It developed that a representative of the Co-ordinating Center had invaded the studio while a program was being taped and had snatched the script out of the announcer's hand. When we reached the studio, we found that the incident had been caused by Sergei Petrovich Melgunov, a white-goateed Russian from Paris who before his involvement with the Americans and émigré politics had been a historian of some distinction. In the face of such challenges, the response of Manning Williams as head of the American advisory staff seemed to be mainly to vacillate. We had to vacillate with him. At his best Williams was to us a man tortured by personal insecurity. In the present circumstances, he probably had good reason to be unsure of support from higher authority in the United States.

The situation spawned absurdities. One was the two competing news departments at the station. The first, headed by a Russian named Kumming who had been appointed by the Co-ordinating Center, ground out wordily propagandistic news items that made even Radio Moscow's bombastic bulletins seem highly professional by comparison. To try to fill the void, Ed Stevens had formed a second news department staffed by émigrés hired for their professional abilities, not their political affiliations. Every day, both news shops produced a complete newscast. We advisors tried to persuade the broadcasters to use as much of the Stevens output as possible, with a face-saving admixture of the least objectionable items from the Kumming outfit. All this took hours of maneuvering and sapped RL's ability to react quickly to events.

Another crippling circumstance was that morale at the station had been shattered even before it went on the air. Back in the fall of the previous year, word had come from the United States to prune the staff drastically. On a single day, December 1, 1952, eighteen American employees and dozens of émigrés were suddenly called into the personnel office, one at a time, and told that they were fired. In the poverty and insecurity of postwar Germany, these incomprehensible actions were particularly grim for the émigré victims. An American in the personnel section who was charged with breaking the news through an interpreter told me that three women had fainted on the floor of his office in the course of this harsh display of American power.

A Russian-speaking American radio producer, George Vicas, was consoling his fiancee, a secretary named Lois McCullough who had just been given her dismissal notice, when he too was summoned to the personnel section to get the same word about himself. Then, after all this carnage, new instructions came, and some of the émigrés on the dismissal list were called back in and told that the whole thing had been a mistake. Only one of the Americans was reinstated, after he literally fell on his knees and begged mercy for himself and his family.

At the time, those who worked at my level had no idea of the reason for the dismissals. But in Washington the star of Senator Joseph McCarthy was on the rise, and we wondered whether our fallen colleagues, many of whom had become close friends, were somehow being suspected of treason, and whether we might be next on the list. Years later, a knowledgeable person in the United States told me that the whole business was the result of bureaucratic infighting in Washington. One faction in the government wanted to go ahead with setting up the broadcasts. The other was resolutely opposed. The balance of power between the two forces shifted from hour to hour. A decision to kill the entire operation had been overturned, but not in time to avert the December purge.

One thing helped to keep the incident vivid in memory despite the passage of the years. A hip New York character who worked on the third floor in production warned those of us who refused to break off our friendship with Vicas: "If you walk like a duck and talk like a duck, people are going to think you're a duck." He stayed with RL for many years but never lived down this remark, for which he was continually repaid by hearing people make little quacking noises whenever he passed by.

For those of us who remained, the damage to morale was devastating. Some of those who had been dismissed fared not too badly. A secretary named Mary Dick, who had been recruited in New York and had spent exactly one week in Munich before being given the gate, took her severance pay, cashed in her first-class return ticket, and spent a year in Rome writing a book. George Vicas and his fiancee Lois used their payoff to stage an elaborate wedding in Davos, Switzerland, which my wife and I attended along with others from RL. Then they returned to New York where George went to work at CBS News for the legendary Edward R. Murrow. Vicas achieved distinction as a producer of radio and later television documentaries, first at CBS and then at NBC, for which in the 1960s he headed an independent production unit based in Paris. One of the ousted émigrés, a fiery Georgian named Alyosha Bogaturia, got financial backing from a Munich brewery and opened a profitable restaurant across the street from RL. Bogaturia had been on the list of employees who were called in and told that their firing was canceled, but by that point he was so indignant that he showered the American personnel officer with colorful expletives and stalked out of his office. His restaurant, which at first had no competition at RL's lonely location, became a major institution in the life of the station, giving Alyosha many opportunities to vent his spleen to its employees and any of their bosses who dared to set foot there.

Those were some of the troubles that set the stage for our meeting in Manning Williams's office on that cold March morning. We now know that the problems of RL in Munich were more than matched by the behind-the-scenes turmoil in Moscow. Stalin had actually had his stroke on the night of March 1, the very day RL had gone on the air. Not until March 4, when it seemed that recovery was hopeless, did his colleagues in the Soviet leadership share the news with the outside world. His daughter Svetlana has described the scene at the suburban dacha where her oxygen-starved father was slowly choking to death, as his top lieutenants dithered between trying to keep the old man alive and plotting their bid for power after his death, while worrying about losing control over the Soviet masses. But at our gathering in Munich, we were certain only of our own disarray.

The drama of the meeting was heightened by constant interruptions. People kept bringing in new DPA dispatches, and the chief monitor descended frequently from his fourth-floor aerie to hand us freshly typed transcripts of the latest Moscow broadcasts.

Without being asked, Shub took over the proceedings. His raucous New York voice cut through the gloom of impotence and inaction.

"This is history in the making. We've got to rise to the occasion." He went through the list of recommendations for action that he had shared with me in the car.

When Manning Williams voiced the objection that we Americans had no authority to order action, Shub brushed it aside impatiently. A small, slight man in his early forties, he strode around the office, peering out malevolently from beneath an unruly shock of black hair. Even to those of us who saw him as a hero, Boris looked slightly sinister, with piercing eyes circled by dark rings, separated by a large pointed nose. He and Manning were friends from an earlier day as U.S. officials in occupied Germany, before the creation of RL, but their temperaments were poles apart. Their relationship had already been strained by Shub's antics in getting RL on the air. Williams saw himself as the final radio authority among us Americans, the one who had the responsibility. He resented, not unreasonably, Shub's free and easy way of giving orders to his staff.

"God damn it, Manning, we've got to do the job. In our whole lives we'll never have another chance like this. There are big changes ahead in the Soviet Union. We can be part of the act, if we stop masturbating. We've got a chance to help them see the truth about their country and the world they live in. But we've got to cut this horse shit." Shub raised his voice tauntingly. "If you fail us, we'll never forgive you. Your kids will never forgive you." Williams flushed angrily. Shub was using his devotion as a father to goad him to action.

We all knew that, if he wanted to, Williams could give orders to the staff by virtue of his control of the payroll. Few would disobey. His hesitation stemmed partly from a residual commitment to the principle of émigré autonomy. Manifestly, another part was fear of what might happen to him if he took authority into his own hands.

The meeting broke up with a half-hearted mandate from Williams to do Shub's bidding. Manning Williams was left slumped nervously in his desk chair. Outside, Shub groaned to Ronalds and me about Williams's penchant for "snatching defeat from the jaws of victory." He railed, "Manning is suffering from delusions of adequacy"—one of his favorite epithets for incompetence. Characteristically, Boris left the building soon afterward to go on a tour of Bavarian castles with his wife Libby. That was his modus operandi: to stir people to action and then leave them to pick up the pieces.

Ed Stevens went back to his office to work on the newscast. Ronalds and I turned our attention to trying to use our influence with the émigré staff to revamp the feature output. Fast-breaking news from Moscow was putting us under pressure to react quickly in the broadcasts. Here, too, we were woefully unprepared. In those first days of RL, the daily program did not even go on the air until early evening, Moscow time. That gave us little leeway, however, because of the time delay in getting the programs to the transmitters.

Our studios in Munich were supposed to feed transmitters in the Rhineland, hundreds of miles away. The method then devised seems antediluvian in today's age of dedicated satellite relays and high-fidelity landlines. It consisted of having a motorcyclist pick up the tapes at the studios in Oberwiesenfeld and rush them through traffic to the Hauptbahnhof, Munich's main railroad station, where they would be given to the conductor of a departing train. On arrival of the train in Mannheim, more than three hours later, the conductor would pass them to a second motorcyclist who would then speed to the transmitter site near the Rhineland village of Lampertheim, another ten miles over country roads. Total time for this operation, when everything clicked, was a good five hours—during which the newscast being broadcast by RL could become hopelessly obsolete. We were acutely aware that Stalin might die at any time, requiring our instant reaction, or that he might live on for days or weeks.

The rest of that day's details are a blur. We had to do a quick remake of the current broadcast and also of the next day's features. Normally, we relied heavily on taped features airmailed from the programming unit Shub had set up in New York on West 47th Street in the heart of the diamond district, where he had assembled some of the best talent available to RL. But now, because of time considerations, we were on our own. I remember tumbling into bed back at the hotel after a postmortem session with Shub, Stevens, and Ronalds in somebody's room.

The next morning, Boris was on the phone again before dawn.

"He's dead, he's really dead. Moscow just announced it."

By now, Stalin's actual death was almost an anticlimax, but it meant that again we had to rush to the studio in Oberwiesenfeld to scrap the existing programs and prepare new ones.

Sometime during the morning, Boris grabbed me as I was dashing down a corridor. He had been listening to Radio Moscow while the rest of us worked, and was dancing with excitement. He shouted at me: "Chopin's *Funeral March!* Dirges from Beethoven! That's how they're mourning Stalin."

I must have looked blank.

"Don't you see? Western composers! No Kabalevsky or the rest of that Stalinist garbage! Something's already changing there!"

At the end of another long, stressful day, we adjourned to Stevens's room for drinks, dinner, and discussion. I left Boris and Ed brooding about RL's shortcomings and fell into bed in my own room, two doors down the hall.

Toward two in the morning, Pat and I were awakened from an exhausted sleep by a knock on the door. The night porter had been sent to tell me to get dressed right away and come up to Otis Swift's suite.

When, mystified, I knocked on Swift's door a few minutes later, he opened it himself, looking haggard and frightened. Sitting in his parlor-office were Shub and Stevens, radiating an air of subdued triumph. It developed that after I had left them they had had a few more drinks, then decided to bypass Manning Williams and go directly up to Swift's suite. There they had spent hours working to convince him that urgent action was needed to avert disaster. Their tactic was naked intimidation, to plant in that rabbity little man the fear that, unless he did as they said, he was in terrible trouble. I was at the center of the plan they unfolded to him. Finally, after hours of agonizing, he capitulated and had me summoned.

So, within the hour, I had packed, kissed Pat good-by, and in the dark was headed up the Autobahn for Lampertheim and the transmitters. With me were three others: a Russian producer who used the Teutonic pseudonym of Wolfgang Koehler to protect his family in Moscow; a former Moscow actor named Sergei Nikolayevich Dubrovsky, whose wonderfully deep and resonant voice coupled with an intelligent delivery made him RL's star announcer ("our answer to Levitan," as Shub put it); and our driver, Ilya Sanets, a delightful Russian wearing a battered beret, who throughout the trip regaled us with farcical stories of his brief career as a French legionnaire.

Our early morning arrival at the transmitter site, in a clearing in the forest, produced unexpected drama. No one had bothered to notify the American manager, a lovable elderly ex–naval officer named Danny Harkins, that we were on the way. Such was the level of insecurity among the staff that, when he saw me step from the car, Danny assumed at once that I had been sent to replace him. I can still see the stricken look on the face of that nice, friendly man. I hastened to reassure him and, relieved, he sat us down to a hospitable breakfast.

From then on, until we were recalled to Munich days later, our routine was the same. At appointed hours, the Munich staff would telephone us in the tiny control room at the transmitter site. As someone read the latest newscast to us over the phone, sentence by sentence, we took turns copying it down in Russian longhand. Then, as Koehler presided, Dubrovsky read the pieces of paper onto tape. That way, RL gained the ability to react to the news within minutes, if necessary. (The concept of live broadcasting was alien to us amateurs in that far-off day.)

Later, Pat confessed to me that after I left Munich she had been worried that long hours and heavy pressures would take their toll on my health. With that on her mind, she happened to run into Otis Peabody Swift in the hotel lobby on the morning of my early departure for Lampertheim. "What was your husband doing in my room last night? What did he want?" Swift questioned her. A strange man.

Pat need not have worried. After the pressure cooker of Munich, the routine at the transmitters was a rest cure. I chafed at being away from the center of things, but there were compensations. The forest around the transmitters imparted a deep sense of peace. We were quartered in a rundown but cozy inn in the village of Lampertheim. I remember soft down comforters and the play of morning sunlight on the cobblestones outside my window. There was a *Stube* where all day and evening the locals came to drink beer and play the card game *Skat*.

It was in that *Stube* that I acquired one of the most bizarre memories of my life. It involved the orations for Stalin's funeral. We had talked the owner, a genial Rhinelander named Herr Bayer, into letting us tune the radio receiver, which usually carried local music, to the shortwave broadcasts of Moscow's Russian-language home service. There we were, in this oh so *gemütlich* setting, listening to dirges from the military bands in Red Square and the eulogies by Malenkov, Molotov, and Beria, all punctuated by the sound of someone playing the pinball machine, as the German beer drinkers stared disgustedly into their glasses.

During our stay in Lampertheim, we came across a khaki sedan cruising the roads near the transmitters. It bore the license plate of the Soviet Military Mission in Bonn, early evidence of official Soviet interest in the new radio station.

If the Kremlin was already taking RL seriously, few others were. Word quickly spread on Munich's civilian and military grapevine that RL lacked a firm hand at the top—witness such quixotic events as the December purge—that a hybrid, headstrong rabble called a "Coordinating Center" was being allowed to interfere with the programs, and that our technical arrangements were a combination of Rube Goldberg and Pony Express. Visitors to our building, used to German punctiliousness, were dismayed by the easy irreverence of our slouching, tatterdemalion staff. It was around this time that some kibitzer nicknamed RL "Radio Hole-in-the-Head."

Decades after these events, it is impossible to recall all the details of RL's early broadcasts. If copies are in storage in some obscure archive, I am unaware of it. In any case, I have no doubt that many of them were clumsy and unprofessional. Yet without the intervention of Boris Shub they would have been far more objectionable. At the very least, Shub had inspired us to cut out the worst of the "garbage," the propagandistic pathos and hyperbole that flowed naturally from the pens of amateur scriptwriters intent on venting deep emotional grievances against the Soviet regime.

RL's success would have been impossible without the talent and dedication of its émigré contributors, but Shub helped to give their efforts cohesiveness and direction. On the American side, Ronalds and I were only two of the young executives touched by Shubian ideas who continued to ask ourselves "what Boris would have done" long after he had left RL. And, although we didn't know it at the time, there were already distant listeners in the Soviet Union who were being touched by the influence of the Shubian vision in those early broadcasts, some of whom later made their way to the West and became RL staffers.

Shub dreamed of a radio voice that could unlock the frozen energy and conscience of a nation whose talents had produced a Pushkin and Tolstoy, a Tchaikovsky and Shostakovich, a Mendeleev and Sikorsky. He believed fervently that a Russia reawakened would, by its own internal dynamic, sweep aside the Soviet system. To him, any crass manipulation by outsiders, any Madison Avenue hectoring, any sloganeering "anti-Commie crap," could only harm that process.

Shub set for the station a pattern of restraint and objectivity, of honesty and devotion to democratic principle that, despite lapses, would sustain it over more than four decades of speaking to Soviet audiences.

Forget the CIA!　2

M any others have written about the Central Intelligence Agency's covert funding of our radio station. Right from the start it was arguably the worst-kept secret in the history of statecraft. Without being told officially, I had heard about the CIA involvement well before I joined Radio Liberty, from a friend who worked in Washington, D.C. Most of my colleagues, and not only the American ones, had heard similar revelations. I doubt that there was a single stoker or sweeper in our building out at Oberwiesenfeld who did not have some inkling of the true state of affairs.

Quite recently I learned some details of RL's prehistory that I had never known before, thanks to a letter in the *Washington Post* (June 24, 1993) from Richard T. Davies, a retired State Department specialist in Soviet affairs who had capped a distinguished career by serving for five years as U.S. ambassador to Poland. His letter was prompted by a *Post* story saying that RL (and Radio Free Europe) "were founded by the CIA." Davies objected to this formulation, saying that it "scants the role of Secretary of State George C. Marshall, the State Department and, in particular, its policy planning staff, headed by George F. Kennan, which was responsible for drafting NSC 58/2, 'United States Policy Toward the Soviet Satellite States of Eastern Europe.'" This document, adopted in November 1949 by the National Security Council, had "initiated the policy pursuant to which the broadcasting operations of RFE and, later, RL, were undertaken," Davies wrote. He added that Kennan–one of the State Department's first Russian specialists and later ambassador to the Soviet Union, who retired to a post at the Institute for Advanced Study at Princeton–had been the "moving spirit" behind establishment of the Office of Special Projects in the State Department, which in 1950 was incorporated into the CIA.

The truth is that the CIA factor, such as it was, made little difference, especially to those of us who were responsible solely for getting the programs on the air. We were left very much to our own devices. If you stop to think about the massive volume of material that goes into a daily broadcast, and the speed with which it must be handled, the instant decisions that must be made, it should be obvious that no agency outside our building could exercise effective control. They had to trust us.

And trust us they did. On rare occasions, when there was a major crisis that had the potential of disturbing world peace, we would receive a brief message through the New York headquarters enjoining us to stick to objective reporting and limit our commentary. By the time the message reached us, it was usually too late to affect the program. In any case, we knew enough not to broadcast inflammatory commentary. In those early decades RL never became embroiled in the kind of worldwide scandal that was triggered by the broadcasts of our fellow station, Radio Free Europe, during the Hungarian crisis of 1956.

That was the situation as long as I stayed in Munich. If we erred, we usually had ourselves to blame, not the CIA. In 1961, the year before I left, I was the American advisor for RL's Russian broadcasts. We learned from news reports that an invasion of Cuba was in progress, ostensibly led by Cuban émigrés. Nobody told us that it was in reality a CIA operation. This was early in President John F. Kennedy's administration. When I saw a news agency item about a "white paper" on the invasion by Arthur Schlesinger, Jr., a respected historian who was one of Kennedy's close advisors, I decided that the invasion must be a spontaneous Cuban action. Accordingly, I persuaded the Russian desk to do a lyrical documentary on the Cuban people's historic love of freedom. Later on, of course, I realized my mistake. The point is that on that occasion RL was subverted not by some directive from on high but by my own ignorance and gullibility. (Still later, when I heard that the invasion had been overseen by one of my old MIT professors, Richard Bissell, who had become a deputy director of the CIA, I had trouble connecting him in that activist role with the dry, colorless individual who on Mondays used to fly up from an undisclosed job in Washington to lecture us undergraduates on national income.)

With regard to RL, the story I have to tell here is one of real people who did their work openly and were ready to answer publicly for their actions. After all, what can be less secret than a radio broadcast? The reader will look in vain here for sensational revelations about the CIA. That is not what this book is about, and I would demean the many devoted men and women who conscientiously put out the broadcasts if I tried to link them with the shadowy world of intelligence. If that detracts from my narrative, so be it.

We called the CIA "the boys," short for "the boys in the back room," I suppose. In later years, one of the "boys" would occasionally be added to the broadcast staff. Such people were effective only if they worked like the rest of us, trying to be responsible journalists. Those who pursued a different agenda were quickly frozen out, and they moved elsewhere.

In large part our long-term independence was due to the integrity and determination of Howland H. Sargeant, a former Rhodes scholar, who succeeded Admiral Stevens as president of our parent "committee" in New York. Sargeant, who remained in that position for two decades, helped to ensure our respectability by winning the consent of former presidents Herbert Hoover and Harry Truman to have their names appear on our letterhead, each as an "honorary chairman." After 1961 a third name was added, that of Dwight Eisenhower. Sargeant reasoned that the names would discourage whoever might seek to have us conduct unsavory activities.

Another of Sargeant's contributions to RL's independence was his instruction to the staff never to engage in anything inconsistent with the activity of a genuine broadcasting organization, and to let him know right away if an employee was approached to do something improper. A former assistant secretary of state who knew his way around the bureaucracy, he was willing to take the heat from Washington.

Sargeant had the additional distinction, in those early days, of being married to the Hollywood actress Myrna Loy, whom many of us had idolized for her roles in the *Thin Man* series and other Hollywood productions. In her autobiography, she recalled our boss as "attractive in a masculine, staunch New England way, possessing the integrity once implied by the designation 'Yankee.'" Even after their divorce, she referred to him as "a marvelous, brilliant man." But Sargeant did not appear on the scene until 1954, and I am getting ahead of my narrative.

The acid test of covering Stalin's death in March 1953 exposed the flaws of our fledgling organization. The "Co-ordinating Center for Anti-Bolshevik Struggle" had demonstrated its incompetence to run RL. The events also revealed that, in the language of the day, RL could be "an important weapon in the Cold War." American management decided to take matters into its own hands.

The Co-ordinating Center remained in existence for a few more years, with periodic attempts to strengthen it. This task was entrusted to a new director of émigré relations, who operated in Munich but separately from RL. He was a lanky Yankee from Gloucester, Massachusetts, named Isaac Patch. Ike Patch was a former foreign service officer who had served in Moscow and the Soviet-occupied Chinese port of Dairen during and right after World War II. While in Dairen with him, his wife had given birth to their second child, delivered by a Soviet navy surgeon who had last performed that operation in 1917. In 1948 Patch and his family had been expelled from Prague on twenty-four hours' notice. A tall, shrewd stringbean with a deceptively mild appearance and manner, Patch with his laid-back style and perennial optimism was ideally suited to the job. In time, however, even he gave up in desperation. His last gasp was a mammoth conference of émigré leaders that he staged at Tegernsee, a picturesque lake resort outside Munich. There he succeeded, but only temporarily, in bringing together two political enemies, both of whom came over from their New York homes for the conference: Alexander Kerensky, head of the Russian provisional government of 1917, and Boris Nikolaevsky, a well-known Menshevik or anti-Stalinist leftist. Kerensky was suspicious that Nikolaevsky was conniving with the non-Russian émigré groups to dismember his beloved Russia, and he withdrew from the proceedings.

Even though we Americans had been given a more active part, it was obvious that RL's indispensable need was for more and better émigré staff. Few of our people had professional journalism backgrounds, let alone radio experience. The American radio experts who had been sent over did not help matters by insisting on a rigid program format with exact five- or ten-minute segments, a pattern that lent itself to commercial radio in the United States but was irrelevant to our broadcasting needs or, for that matter, to those of any European country.

Even more important, the staff lacked political maturity and basic creative talent. Once again, Boris Shub leaped into the breach. Shortly after Stalin's funeral, he left Munich on an energetic talent hunt through France and England, combing the Russian émigré communities there.

Boris's visit to England produced a story that I heard again and again in later years, whenever I visited that country. It was always told with wide-eyed horror. It seems that Boris stormed breathlessly into the book-lined Oxford study of Isaiah Berlin (later Sir Isaiah), one of the gods of British scholarship, who had been born into a Russian-speaking family in Riga. He found Berlin, who possessed something of a reputation for pomposity and self-importance, sitting comfortably near a cozy fire.

"Berlin," he shouted (according to the many versions of the story that I heard), "we want you to come to Munich to write scripts for Radio Liberation!"

Recoiling from this outburst, Berlin answered with frosty British politeness: "I'm terribly sorry, Mr. Shub, but you see I have my books here, my students. I'm afraid I'm not interested."

"Come on, Berlin, how much do they pay you here? Whatever it is, we'll double it."

The story always ended there. Actually, Boris was quite impressed by what he saw in England. When we met him at the Munich airport on his return, he got off the plane saying, "I've just been in a sane asylum."

Who was Boris Shub?

This volatile New York intellectual had been raised on Russian politics by a socialist father who had emigrated to the United States before the revolution. The family apartment in New York was a meetingplace for émigré politicians, often of conflicting views. According to a family story, Boris at age three had made an early political decision by refusing to shake hands with a visitor—Leon Trotsky. Later, he won a degree from City College, then in its academic heyday, and went on to law school at Columbia University. The young man who emerged from this eclectic upbringing was equally at home with, and passionately devoted to, the Russian humanism of Leo Tolstoy and Alexander Herzen and the democracy of Thomas Jefferson. Somewhere in the mix of his intellectual formation was the influence of an austere rabbinical grandfather who had turned him against religious forms but not without helping to make him a compulsive preacher and teacher.

With this background, Boris was a natural for political communication. As a GI during World War II, he was assigned to Radio Luxemburg, a "black" propaganda station operated clandestinely by the U.S. Army, which pretended to be an anti-Nazi radio broadcasting to German soldiers from behind their own lines. Discharged from the army at war's end, he soon returned to Germany as political advisor for Radio in the American Sector (RIAS) in Berlin. As a postwar broadcaster, he showed an ability to reach audiences in Soviet-occupied Germany that grew in importance with the intensification of the Cold War.

The Berlin years were seminal for Shub. RIAS became a nerve center of political and intellectual life linking the two Germanys, East and West. In those days before erection of the Berlin Wall, this Russian-speaking American roamed the streets of the East Sector, talking wherever he could with Soviet personnel. What he learned inspired him to write a book, *The Choice,* which became part of the rationale for those who helped to found RL. In *The Choice* Shub argued that war with the Soviet Union was not inevitable, as many then feared, and that the West should try to reach out to the Russian people through the democratic and humanitarian elements of their own prerevolutionary tradition so as to join forces with them against dictatorship.

To appreciate Shub's feat in steering RL into the role of an honest information medium, it helps to recall that in 1953, the year the station went on the air, U.S. society was in the throes of anti-Communist hysteria, fanned by demagogues like Senator Joseph McCarthy and, in the House of Representatives, by the Un-American Activities Committee. In that Red-baiting atmosphere, any counsel of reasoned moderation was apt to be branded as cowardly or, worse, pro-Soviet.

Shub's tactic in dealing with people was to needle them into an explosion of sincere feeling, to get at the person inside. He used that tactic on me. On his arrival in Munich in the days before Stalin's death, I had been assigned to assist him in various ways. After a few days of being the butt of his caustic wisecracks, I suddenly turned and leveled a stream of obscenities at him. Instead of complaining to higher authority, as I feared when I regained my temper, Boris patted me on the back encouragingly and said, "*That's* the way to go, boy. That's the way." The incident broke the ice between us, and I became his Munich confidant. I was present on another occasion when Boris goaded the usually softspoken Ed Stevens into such a white heat of rage that he screamed at him, "Go fuck yourself, Boris!" and stormed from the room.

Boris called being Jewish in American society "a disability, like having a withered arm," but he never turned his back on his origins.

He was particularly attached to the Yiddish language and culture. Once when we were listening to an RL broadcast that contained a brief excerpt in Yiddish, his eyes filled with tears. "Now there's a language," he told me, all choked up. One of the important influences in his life was his father, David Shub, the noted biographer of Lenin who wrote regularly for the New York Yiddish newspaper *Forverts* as well as for *Novoe Russkoe Slovo* and other Russian publications. Given this background, I was astonished one day to hear Boris inveighing against the state of Israel.

"How come?" I asked him.

"Because Israel is stifling Yiddish culture."

This was his objection to the priority being given in Israel to use of Hebrew. Boris's anti-Zionism was, in any case, largely intellectual and stemmed in part from his socialist heritage, the idea that all nationalism was the enemy of solidarity. I am sure that if Israel's enemies had ever come close to their goal of driving the country into the sea, Boris would have been right there to defend his fellow Jews.

Shub's commitment to politics was matched by his attachment to major league baseball. He had been known to go to Yankee Stadium at four in the morning to assure a seat for an important game, accompanied by his older sister Mona and little brother "Tolya." (Anatole Shub later became Moscow bureau chief of the *Washington Post*.) In his mind, his twin passions were fused. He could interpret complex ideological questions in baseball terms, and vice versa. In my life I have known only one other such virtuoso of politics and baseball, the Harvard historian Adam Ulam, but Ulam is a Red Sox fan.

Although a city boy, Boris was fascinated by horseback riding. Once at a late-night party in Berlin where drinks were served, he fell into conversation with some British cavalry officers, to whom he mentioned that he liked horses. Before he knew it, he had agreed to meet the officers early the next morning for a canter. He had in fact been on a horse only a few times in his life, in Central Park. His wife Libby tried to talk him out of the encounter, but his hubris had taken over. In the morning, she got up to go to the stable with him and watched the awful scene as the party took off. Boris's squat figure was bounced from one end of his horse to the other, as the Britishers trotted crisply next to him in wordless dismay. Boris would tell the story on himself, but Libby told it better. When we laughed at it in Munich in those days, none of us dreamed that Boris's attraction for horseback riding would lead years later to tragedy.

Despite the fiasco of his meeting with Isaiah Berlin, Boris did not return to us empty-handed from his French and British junket. A few weeks later a portly middle-aged gentleman in an elegant dark suit and bowler showed up at RL from Paris. It was the eminent Russian art historian Wladimir Weidle (as he spelled his name in Western languages), author of the book *Russia, Absent and Present* and many other works of intellectual history and literary criticism. Weidle was one of a group of prominent intellectuals who had been expelled by the Soviet authorities in 1923, which probably saved their lives from Stalin's later purges. This gentle, cosmopolitan man was completely at home in Russian, French, German, and English (although he had a slight stammer in all those languages). He was a passionate admirer of the British political system. His bowler and British accent (polished during a stay at Oxford) led my wife, who adored him, to refer to him irreverently as "Jeeves." He once told her that as a Russian of German origin who had been well treated during his asylum in France, he was grateful to all those cultures, "but for England I would die." Libby Shub, who was taken by Weidle on a tour of Venice art treasures, told us that it was one of the most memorable experiences of her life.

Weidle was quickly ensconced as program director at RL. He treated the representatives of the Co-ordinating Center with courtesy and respect, but it was clear that he ran his own shop. A few years later he tired of the endless bickering and give-and-take of getting programs on the air and returned to his Paris home. The time in Munich, however, was not wasted. His presence in those critical early days had been a guarantee that standards of integrity, maturity, and decency would be observed. Without Shub's initiative and magnetism, I doubt that we would ever have had the privilege of having Weidle at RL. Weidle continued to write brilliant programs for us from Paris. He died there many years later, a very old man who had continued right to the end to publish a vast array of articles, ranging from political commentary to film reviews.

Another Shub prize was Victor Frank, who had been head of the British Broadcasting Corporation's prestigious Russian-language service. We newcomers to the world of international broadcasting were increasingly finding our inspiration in the subtle magic of the BBC, whose programs were easily audible in Munich in English, Russian, and a variety of other languages. (I had begun listening to the BBC as a teenager on an isolated farm in New York state, but never dreamed

that I would someday have a professional interest in its work.)
Although a British subject, Frank had been born in Russia, son of the
well-known philosopher Semyon Frank, a Jewish convert to Russian
Orthodoxy, who with his family was another of those who had been
expelled from Soviet Russia in 1923. Victor had been married twice,
both times to Irish women, and like his father he was a convert, in his
case from Russian Orthodoxy to Roman Catholicism.

Somehow, probably because in those days salaries at the BBC
were pathetically small, Shub managed to lure Frank away from his
job, and he joined us in the key position of head of the Russian desk.
Victor, then in his forties, was a deft, seasoned editor and kindly but
firm disciplinarian. He also broadcast his own talks, as he had done at
the BBC. Victor was an anglicized product of the Russian intellectual
tradition. To me, he combined the best of both cultures, with overtones of rabbinical wisdom and wit. As a younger man, he had had a
minor stroke, which he attributed to the shock of his father's death.
He recovered completely, except that one side of his face was slightly
twisted, leaving him with a permanently wry, rather rakish grin. None
of this diminished his considerable attractiveness to the opposite sex.

Not the least of Frank's contributions at RL was helping people
like Ronny Ronalds and me to bridge the professional, linguistic, and
social gap between the émigré and American worlds. Until his advent
we had been pretty much alone in doing this.

Some of the changes after Stalin's death promised hope for a better future in the Soviet Union. Ed Stevens and his Russian wife Nina
began to dream of returning to Moscow, where they still owned a
house. It was clear that Ed's work with RL would not further that
ambition, and they soon left us.

In any case, Ed was not happy living in one room at the Regina-
Palast Hotel with Nina and a small, flatulent white dog named
Pupchik. I remember one evening hearing Ed's plaintive voice raised
to a whine as he and Nina passed the door of our room on their way
to take Pupchik for a walk: "Nina, Nina, on portit ves' vozdukh!"
(Nina, Nina, he pollutes the whole environment!)

In his Munich days Ed was a tall, slender, athletic figure who usually wore a ski cap, which Boris saw as an affectation, leading him to
dub Ed, derisively, "Komsomolets" (an allusion to the young Communist fanatics of the early Soviet period). We Americans all envied his
good Russian. Sometime after leaving Munich, the Stevenses did man-
age to return more or less permanently to Moscow, where Ed worked

as a correspondent for British and U.S. newspapers. He stayed there, almost without interruption, until his death. I did not see him again until more than twenty years later, at a reception in the National Hotel in Moscow. By that time he had aged and had gained so much weight that I barely recognized him. Rumors spread, perhaps baselessly, that the Stevenses were in cahoots with the KGB. When these reached Ed, he denied them, but an American visitor to Moscow in those days told me of talking at a reception with the poet Andrei Voznesensky, a borderline dissident. When Nina Stevens walked up, Voznesensky turned white and fled in evident fear or revulsion, my friend said.

After the Stevenses' departure from Munich, Ronny Ronalds was asked to take over the news department. Ronalds was already demonstrating the qualities that later made him the dominant figure at RL. One such quality was his ability to provide leadership to our émigré colleagues. After years of being pushed around by Soviet, German, and occupation officials, they appreciated this enthusiastic, dapper young American—Ronalds could have modeled Brooks Brothers suits, I am sure—who showed an interest in each of them personally, who was willing to take extra time to listen to the life history of each and their program ideas, and who socialized with them as an equal at parties, where he sang their songs and danced their dances.

Unfortunately, the same lighthearted disposition and unassuming manner that shaped Ronalds's appeal to the émigrés were apt to create the wrong initial impression at the upper levels of the U.S. bureaucracy, especially at the New York headquarters. Back home, executives were expected to "master the art of talking in a deep voice and looking important at meetings," as I complained in a letter about some of Ronalds's troubles written in 1958 to Boris Shub, who was then back in New York. In time Ronalds won out over his critics: his leadership skills and his background in journalism and Russian affairs, combined with an instinctive ability to empathize with Soviet audiences, earned the respect of all of us who were close to the programming operation, and that respect was eventually communicated upward through the hierarchy. In particular, Howland Sargeant became one of Ronalds's great admirers.

That all came later, however, with the growth of the headquarters bureaucracy. Following his assignment in 1953 as head of the news department, Ronalds began to assemble an able—and colorful—staff. One of his windfalls from Shub's Paris-London trip was a novelist-cum-taxi-driver named Gaito Gazdanov, who had been strongly recommended for the station by Wladimir Weidle. Gazdanov and Weidle's wife had risked their lives together in the French Resistance during the war. The Russian-born critic Marc Slonim, writer of a regular literary column for the *New York Times Book Review,* was a great admirer and close friend of Gazdanov, who had helped him as a Jew to escape from France. Gazdanov had published successfully in several languages, including English, but was still driving his cab. A short but wiry and ferocious man with large bushy eyebrows and a rasping voice, on the job he always carried the crank of the cab in his side pocket to deal with recalcitrant passengers. His book *Nochnyye dorogi* (Night Roads), a fictionalized treatment of his experiences at the wheel, is peopled with a wonderful assortment of agents de police, whores, bums, and other characters. Unfortunately, it has never been translated from Russian, though after the collapse of the Soviet Union, a Moscow publisher brought out it and other works by Gazdanov.

Gazdanov had been invited after the war to pay a brief visit to his New York publisher. He told the story of being interviewed by an immigration inspector on his arrival at Ellis Island. The interview went like this, in Gazdanov's telling:

"What do you do for a living, Mr. Gazdanov?"

"I write books."

"Where do you live?"

"In Paris."

"Oh, then you write books in French?"

"No, I write them in Russian."

"Well, if you live in Paris I can't understand why you would write books in Russian."

Finally, tiring of this line of questioning, Gazdanov burst out: "Listen, you idiot, if I were a Communist spy I wouldn't come to this country with a Nansen passport, I'd have an American passport." (Nansen passports were travel documents issued by the League of Nations to refugees after World War I.)

Gazdanov was immediately placed in a detention cell, from which he was released only when his publisher came to Ellis Island to intercede for him.

Ronalds hired Gazdanov for the news desk, where he demonstrated a flair for short, crisp sentences, a knack then unknown to most of our writers. Gazdanov's father was from Ossetia, an Iranian region of the North Caucasus, which since the Soviet breakup of 1991 has been a thorn in the side of both Russia and Georgia. That may help to explain the toughness that enabled the son to drive a Paris cab at night. "Georgii Ivanovich," as he was called in Munich, had himself grown up in St. Petersburg and was one of the station's better Russian stylists. Fortunately for us, the Paris years had taught him to sublimate his native ferocity into ridicule, and some of his witticisms became classics in our little community.

Another member of the Russian literary colony in Paris was also brought to the station by Ronalds. As a young man, Alexander Bacherach had in the 1920s hobnobbed with Ilya Ehrenburg on the terrace of the Rotonde in Montparnasse before Ehrenburg's return to Moscow to achieve a fame of sorts. During the war Bacherach had been secretary to the Nobel Prize winner Ivan Bunin and had shared Bunin's harsh living conditions–and his rations–in the south of France. Bacherach, in his youth a penniless, happy-go-lucky bohemian, had married a beautiful Finn named Kirsti, daughter of a cabinet minister, and had begun to practice a bourgeois lifestyle. His good English and passion for playing bridge gave him better social access to the Munich American community than most of our émigré colleagues enjoyed.

Bacherach shared Gazdanov's caustic wit. Between them they converted the news desk into a nickname factory. I remember that two of our stiffnecked American executives became known to the émigré staff as Bald Ape and Tortoise, names that were well suited to their activity and appearance.

From England, Ronalds brought to Munich a young man named Valerian Obolensky who had been a simultaneous interpreter with the United Nations and had also done Russian jazz programs for the BBC. Known to everyone as Zhuk (Beetle) because of his smooth black hair and brows, a legacy of Caucasian princely ancestry, the handsome, urbane Obolensky was one of the few people I have ever met who was truly bilingual in English and Russian, speaking either language flawlessly and elegantly. In short order he became number two to Ronalds in the news operation. Zhuk and his beautiful young Russian wife, the star announcer of the Munich branch of the Voice of America, were an adornment to any party and one of the most popular couples in our hybrid social world.

When Obolensky emigrated to the States and joined the RL staff in New York, Ronalds replaced him with a Russian-born Pole from

London named Wytold Ryser, whom we all called "Victor." During the war Ryser had been in the diplomatic service of the Polish government in exile, and had then worked for United Press in London, writing diplomatic dispatches. Meeting him was a revelation for me. Until then, the only Poles I had known were steelworkers from Pittsburgh and autoworkers from Detroit with whom I had served in the navy, rough fellows who liked to drink bad liquor and carried knives. Ryser, his British tailoring and dapper mustache impeccable, would bow gracefully from the waist to kiss ladies' hands. In his sleeve he carried not a knife but a handkerchief, which he would withdraw with a flourish. He was at home in more languages than I can remember.

With Weidle as program director, Frank as head of the Russian Desk, and Ronalds running news, I was assigned to what was then called the "information section" and began a new series of adventures, but that is a topic for another chapter.

After these changes in staffing, we were better equipped to weather future crises. These soon came. The struggle for power among Stalin's heirs, culminating in the arrest and execution of Lavrentii Beria, chief of the secret police; the emergence of Nikita Khrushchev as top leader; Khrushchev's reforms and 1956 speech unmasking Stalin's crimes; the ouster of the "anti-Party group" of leading figures for conspiring to overthrow Khrushchev; the removal as minister of defense of the war hero Marshal Georgii Zhukov: all these events whetted Soviet listeners' appetites for accurate information about what was going on in their country and challenged our ability to provide it. Beyond the Soviet borders, there were the 1953 East Berlin uprising, the 1956 Polish and Hungarian crises, and the Suez conflict, all of which exacerbated Soviet-American tensions. These were indeed exciting times to be in the business of broadcasting to Soviet listeners.

In those frantic early days, most of us were hardly aware that RL was also broadcasting in languages other than Russian. The presence in the corridors and studios of Belorussians, Tatars, Caucasians, and Central Asians seemed a sentimental aberration, with no real bearing on the job at hand. Besides, almost all these people spoke Russian. Why couldn't their fellows back home just listen to our Russian broadcasts?

The Soviet Union appeared to us to be a monolith dominated by Russians who were ineluctably supplanting other languages and cultures and replacing them with their own. It was only a matter of time before Soviet society would be ethnically homogeneous. True, Stalin was a Georgian, but he had pursued a policy of russification for years.

In many of us, there was also a certain personal bias. I was a case in point. I had thrown myself into study of the Russian language, become infatuated with my ability to read Pushkin and other authors in the original, and fallen under the spell of the charismatic Russian émigrés who were my teachers. If there was an argument to be made for broadcasting to the Soviet Union in any other language, I had no desire to be part of it. It took another decade for me to realize the error of my orientation.

In Munich, the thankless and essentially impossible task of watching over the non-Russian-language services, more than a dozen of them, was entrusted to Trude Gunther, a tall, cosmopolitan German who had emigrated to the United States before the war because she could not stomach the Nazis. That a woman was given the job in those sexist days reflects, I think, the low priority assigned to it. Trude's main qualification appeared to be that she had taught German at Vassar and Wellesley and had befriended Manning Williams and his wife while working for the American Military Government in Berlin. At the same time, we had to admit that she was a serious person who worked hard and conscientiously. Many of the broadcasters in her jurisdiction were Muslims, but if they objected to her as a woman they held their tongues. Perhaps they sensed that, if Trude left, American management would be capable of replacing her with someone far less decent.

Indeed, in a few years a man was sent out from New York and placed over Trude and the non-Russians. He assembled the staff and made a pompous, self-important speech that was also slightly menacing. One of the German secretaries circulated a hilariously satirical version around the building. The newcomer never recovered from being a laughingstock and soon returned permanently to the United States, leaving the field to Trude. She kept her position until retirement.

Trude's schoolmarmish manner made it difficult for some colleagues to get along with her. One of her assistants was an aged Russian of German origin, Georgii von Stackelberg, who before the war had been a respected Orientalist in Leningrad. Someone once asked Stackelberg how he like working for Trude.

"Every morning when I drag myself to work," he replied, "I congratulate myself for having such good nerves."

Looking back, it seems incredible that for years, while we were carefully screening every word of the Russian broadcasts before they went on the air to control quality, RL was transmitting programs in other languages that in Munich could be understood only by the authors and might, for all we knew in those days of spy mania, have been devastatingly subversive to RL and its sponsors.

Class Conflicts 3

There were two worlds at Radio Liberty, American and émigré. For the most part, the inhabitants of those worlds lived separately from, and in ignorance of, one another. Those Americans with direct radio responsibilities, such as Ronny Ronalds, Trude Gunther, or myself, tried to hover between the two worlds, but we never succeeded in bringing them together.

In their suites of offices on the second floor of the Oberwiesenfeld building, the American top executives were for the most part a shadowy presence, seen only when they emerged to be driven home or to lunch by their chauffeurs. For most of the American administrative employees, regardless of rank, RL meant a world where you ate meals at the American officers club in the Haus der Kunst or at one of the army-run hotels, shopped at the PX, and spent weekends at army recreational facilities in the Alps, where the cost of an all-day ticket for the ski lift was one dollar. In those early years the lowliest American employee, provided that he or she was in the magical category of being a "dollar employee" (meaning those paid in dollars rather than Deutschemark), enjoyed access to these privileges. It is hard to blame people in a strange land for wanting to be with their fellow citizens, but this lifestyle did not help to narrow the gap between the Americans and others. The disparity was compounded by a dual salary scale, "American" and "local," under which RL's chief producer, probably the highest paid local employee, earned less than an American secretary. Those with local salaries were acutely aware of this difference. (With perhaps poetic justice, people who stayed with RL through the years saw the tables turn, as local Deutschemark salaries appreciated and the dollar dropped in value, to the point where in later years, when I came back to Munich as a visitor, I felt like a poor relation.)

The socioeconomic gap, plus deep cultural differences and the inability of most Americans, particularly at the top, to communicate in any language but English, helped keep the two worlds apart. While the Americans were doing their own thing, the Russians and others lived in a quasi-Soviet universe whose values were composed of the difference between Moscow and Vologda, or between the World War II emigration and the earlier "White Guard" emigration, or whether the old-fashioned word for "English," *aglitskii,* was as proper as the modern *angliiskii.* These worlds, American and émigré, were like two grindstones spinning independently on the same axle, separated by a narrow gap but never touching. A few of us who could speak both English and Russian (the lingua franca of the émigrés, regardless of nationality) and thus could communicate with both worlds were charged by management with trying to bring the émigré wheel into synch with the American one, which was supposed to be the driver. We never succeeded. If we tried too hard, we ourselves usually ended up being ground between the two stones.

There were comical aspects to this situation. If the Americans were ignorant of the émigré world, the émigrés had ways of penetrating the American higher echelon. Every American top or middle-level executive had a car with a driver. Most of the drivers were Russian or of some other Soviet nationality. For the most part, the drivers understood more English than their bosses realized. As a result, few things escaped the notice of the émigrés. I remember a morning when one of the American middle-level executives came to my office, white-faced, and told me he was going to be fired.

"Are you sure?" I asked. "How do you know?"

"My driver told me," he gasped. Sure enough, the same day his superior called him in and told him the bad news. I remembered this experience years later when I visited the U.S. Embassy in Moscow and heard U.S. diplomats talking freely about sensitive matters while being chauffeured around the city by their Soviet drivers, the latter almost surely reporting to the KGB.

At RL in those postwar days, the post of driver for an American was a highly desirable job. First, there were many opportunities for overtime. Americans would use their drivers for weekend trips for themselves and their families, to visit baroque Bavarian castles or outlying porcelain and glass factories. This was considered a routine perquisite for those of high rank, and RL picked up the bill. Second, Americans often became attached to their drivers and were generous about illegally sharing scarce goods from the PX, contraband in the German economy. This latter practice produced one amusing incident.

An American from RL named Forsberg, a man with a dry sense of humor, was being taken to the PX by a Russian driver, an oxlike man named Repnin.

"Can I pick up anything for you?" he asked magnanimously.

"As a matter of fact, Mr. Forsberg," Repnin replied, "German condoms are terrible. Could you get some American ones for me?"

"Sure, how many do you want?"

"Well, I don't get this chance very often. Could you get me quite a few?"

In the PX Forsberg walked over to a counter where a bored German salesperson was placidly chewing her gum.

"Some condoms, please."

"Yes, sir, how many?" she replied languidly.

"Give me a gross."

The gum chewing stopped. "A gross? Isn't that an awful lot?"

Forsberg had a sudden inspiration. "I know," he explained, "we're having a party." He left the sales clerk staring after him openmouthed.

In Munich American administrators drew up elaborate organizational charts, mainly for their superiors back in the United States. The charts always showed a neat pyramid of authority with the president of the committee at the top, his senior lieutenants under him, and the junior Americans somewhere in the middle, followed by the émigré supervisors and, at the bottom, the actual broadcasters. The idea, of course, was that the president issued directives that were implemented meticulously by successive echelons of those below. In practice, this ideal chain of command functioned less and less effectively as one got near the bottom. For people such as Ronalds and myself, who were supposed to pass on American directives to the émigrés under us, it was sheer fantasy. Instead of pushing buttons and issuing orders that were instantly obeyed, as our superiors imagined us doing, we had to beg, coax, and wheedle. We could sometimes influence but never fully control. It's a good thing that we understood the limits of our real authority: had we Americans really tried to take decision-making power into our own hands, our broadcasts would have been disastrous. Even those of us who knew the language fairly well were not Soviet Russians (or Ukrainians or Georgians), and we lacked the intimate knowledge of the audience that was indispensable for intelligent communication.

As a rule, the top executives never found out how little actual power they had over the broadcasts. Lacking knowledge of the languages, they were forced to rely on English-language summaries of the contents, which, naturally, were tailored by those charged with preparing them to give the top brass what they wanted to hear. The American executives went about their work in the sublime belief that they were running things. The reality was much different: the main function of most of them was to keep their bosses happy back home, thus assuring the continuing flow of money. As for the rest of us, we asked only that the brass not interfere with the broadcasting effort.

One anomaly of international broadcasting bureaucracies has always amazed me. The closer an employee is to the actual broadcasts, to the microphone and the audience, the lower his or her status is on the organizational charts. Those whose voices are heard every day in the "target" country are in effect the peasants of the operation. Conversely, those who sit in big corner offices and draw high salaries, whatever their value administratively, have relatively little to do with the product that actually goes on the air, the lifeblood of the whole activity. That is true of Radio Liberty, Radio Free Europe, Voice of America, the BBC, and any of the many other international radios with which I have had contact. If those efforts are effective at all, and some are much less so than others, then it is a tribute to the dedication of the lowly broadcasters.

Those sophisticated émigrés who came to us in Munich with French or British passports (and American PX cards) in their pockets were a small minority in the building at Oberwiesenfeld. Most of the writers and announcers, and nearly all the people who performed lesser duties, had *staatenlos* (stateless) stamped in their German documents. In pay and privilege, these "new émigrés" made up a kind of netherworld at the station, with its own values and shibboleths. To them, the rest of us were the *nachal'stvo,* a class-conscious collective noun for "boss." The word had acquired special notoriety in Soviet society as a designation for the new and unloved Communist elite, and its application to us American executives was not flattering.

The stateless lived in displaced persons' (DP) camps around Munich, which had been set up after the war by the military government. Before every shift at RL, Volkswagen minibuses went from Oberwiesenfeld to camps in the outlying villages of Karlsfeld, Ludwigsfeld, and Schleissheim to bring employees to work. In the DP camps conditions were spartan, but Communist and Nazi brutalities were a thing of the past. Moreover, the people who lived there had managed somehow to escape the massive roundup staged by the Americans and British at war's end to return Soviet citizens to Stalin's control—an action taken partly in the mistaken belief that its victims were all "war criminals," partly out of a sense of duty toward a wartime ally that was soon to be repaid by the Kremlin with hostility and threats. Of those who had not been so fortunate, hundreds committed suicide on the way "home," correctly anticipating that what awaited them was either slow death in the gulag or more rapid death by execution.

Our building at Oberwiesenfeld was haunted by the memory of other, earlier camps in which so many of the employees had been inmates. There was the gulag, from which prisoners had been released to the Red Army to fight against Nazi invaders. Then came the German prisoner of war camps filled during the war with two classes of prisoners: those taken in combat and the large numbers of deserters from the Soviet regime. There were also the *Ostarbeiter* camps, for civilians brought forcibly from German-occupied parts of the Soviet Union to work for the Nazi war effort. Those who "sat" in the camps had previously, like all Soviet citizens, undergone the ravages of collectivization and famine. Many had lost their families in the purges and the war. Some of the DP barracks sported jaunty window boxes with geraniums, but there was an overall atmosphere of tragedy and hopelessness, with a high incidence of alcoholism.

Former Soviet citizens who had stayed in Germany after the war tended to live in a world of their own, a world that resented the "old émigrés," those of their fellow countrymen who, like Wladimir Weidle and Victor Frank, had managed to get away, most of them soon after the 1917 Bolshevik seizure of power, to build a good life in the West. This resentment stemmed partly from envy, partly from the feeling that their more fortunate compatriots were incapable of understanding what they had been through and looked down on them as proletarian rabble.

I remember a nasty little one-on-one altercation. Lolly L'vov (he spelled it "Livoff") was a fiery oldster with a nicotine-stained white goatee who had lived in France before the war and was said—though never accused of war crimes—to have conducted militant anti-Bolshevik propaganda in the German-occupied part of the Soviet Union. Lev Korneichuk was a young ex-Soviet officer who had fought in the Red Army and had defected to the West only after the Germans had been beaten. I happened to be present when their paths crossed one day in the station library. The exchange was brief but bitter:

"Sovetskaya svoloch!" (Soviet son of a bitch!)

"Belogvardeyets!" (White Guardist!)

Whether the old émigrés had collaborated with the Germans or fought on the side of the Western allies seemed to make little difference. The social generation gap was the same. The DPs accused the Westernized émigrés of having gained their status at RL by being toadies to us Americans, of using their knowledge of English and manners to curry favor with us.

The world of the new émigrés had its own uncrowned king, an extraordinary Russian named Leonid Pylayev.

Pylayev was the ultimate nontoady. Every day this former activist of the Komsomol, the Soviet youth organization, who had become a gulag inmate and then German prisoner, held court seated in a corner of RL's canteen surrounded by rapt male admirers. From that throne he would deliver a monologue, acted out with obscene gestures and punctuated by gales of laughter from his audience. His frequent target was the station's upper crust.

Pylayev had a classic comedic face. In repose it was tinged with sadness, like a clown's mask. Yet it conveyed the feeling that laughter was not far off, that its owner was about to be victim, or perhaps to make someone else the victim, of some hilarious pratfall, physical or verbal. Great comedians like Charlie Chaplin or Fernandel have had such faces. Lurking in them is a kind of implied threat to the dignity of their social superiors, to the stuffy rigidity that when punished by laughter forms, according to the French philosopher Henri Bergson, the basis of all humor.

In Pylayev's case, the face had been forged by exposure in Stalin's and Hitler's camps. It had myriad tiny creases, explained to me by other camp veterans as the result of searing winter gales, that enhanced the peasant coarseness that was an essential part of Pylayev's public image.

I never knew how much of Pylayev's rough manners and crude language was affectation. We learned early at RL not to press people—already resentful of the *Fragebogen* (written questionnaire) imposed on them by the bureaucrats of the military government—for details of a past that might be painful or embarrassing. Of Pylayev it was said that he had been brought up by two aunts, refined and respectable Russian ladies. On those occasions when he wanted to be serious, he could produce a literate, intelligent piece of writing. But if he had ever read Tolstoy or Turgenev, he never admitted it. In public, his stock in trade was the unpublished masterpieces of Russian pornography, epics such as *Luka Mudishchev,* a work whose authorship is as unknown as that of the English language's dirty limericks and a telling hint of the rich life behind the official front of Soviet culture.

Fortunately for RL, the same talent that kept the canteen hangers-on in stitches also made of Pylayev a peerless broadcaster. Part of his genius was the ability to project his comic persona aurally to listeners who could not see his face. Whenever the tape of one of his regular talks was played in an audition room at RL, people from all over the building would leave work to crowd around the open door and listen, chuckling. Pylayev was unquestionably our most effective voice for reaching rank-and-file Soviet citizens.

We had no systematic audience research in those days, but as word began to trickle back from inside the Soviet Union through scant reports of travelers who had met listeners, "Ivan Ivanovich Oktyabrev" (Pylayev's radio character) usually received top mention. His humor was universal. I can remember seeing the highbrow Victor Frank (frequent butt of Pylayev's populist diatribes in the canteen), his eyes filled with tears of laughter.

The fictional Ivan Ivanovich Oktyabrev was born in October or November 1952 as we were looking frantically for talent and ideas to begin the broadcasts. George Vicas was the midwife.

One day Vicas dropped into my office with a ginger-haired Russian and invited me to audition a tape. We listened to a monologue by a man speaking with the heavy peasant accent of the Volga region, where people say *o* when other Russians say *a.*

The speaker on the tape, identifying himself as "Ivan Ivanovich Oktyabrev" (a whimsical surname derived from the word for October, hallowed month of the 1917 revolution), went through a droll rigamarole. He introduced himself as a "conscientious Soviet citizen" (the words a hackneyed phrase of official propaganda) and "former tractor- and tank-driver" who had landed in the West after falling prisoner to the German army. In the course of the talk, he managed to poke fun at the Soviets, the Germans, and the Western allies. Only later did I understand that, for ordinary Soviet citizens, this was Everyman, his words and intonation a manifesto of shared experience.

At the end of the tape, Vicas looked at me expectantly. Trying to collect my thoughts, I muttered something in English about not being sure that we could get away with making fun of the allied occupying powers. George relayed the gist of my comment in Russian to his ginger-haired companion.

"Are you crazy?" Suddenly the Russian had grabbed me by the shoulders and was sputtering in my face.

"Who are you?"

"Who am I? I'm Pylayev, the author of this broadcast, that's who. What makes you think there's anything wrong with it?"

I backed down to the extent of promising to play the tape for others, and the rest is history, the launching of Pylayev as RL's star performer. (The only reward that Vicas received for his contribution was to be fired on December 1, one of the victims of the purge of Americans.)

The Oktyabrev series was memorable because it generated the first fan mail ever received by RL from the Soviet Union. After going on the air in March 1953 the station, desperate for some response, began broadcasting an appeal for mail, asking listeners to write to a mailbox in West Berlin. For more than a year, we waited fruitlessly. A few letters came in, but they were from lonely Russian émigrés in Belgium and France who had picked up the programs from the "back lobe" of our antennas at Lampertheim. Then one day came a postcard with a Soviet stamp and the postmark of the railroad post office in Brest, on the Soviet-Polish border. At Oberwiesenfeld, the excitement was intense. The message was brief: "Greetings to Ivan Ivanovich Oktyabrev." Two signatures were illegible. We theorized that the card had been sent by Soviet soldiers passing through Brest on the way to or from the Soviet garrison in East Germany.

Oktyabrev's satire was low key. Posing as a zealous but naive Soviet citizen, he would echo the latest propaganda slogans, but with a slightly crazy twist. I remember one of his talks that aired shortly after Stalin's death when *Pravda* had published a solemn editorial calling for a special "Pantheon" in which top Soviet leaders would be given a heroic burial. Speaking with the artificial enthusiasm that Soviet citizens were required to feign at compulsory meetings held to give unanimous endorsement to the party line, Oktyabrev intoned: "As a conscientious Soviet man, I support this latest proposal of our beloved leadership. I should like to propose a slogan in its behalf: 'Better tombs for better leaders.'"

Embattled Soviet dissidents loved Oktyabrev's wit, we later found out. It was a refreshing letup from the heavy-handedness which characterized most propaganda of that day, Western as well as Communist.

My idol Boris Shub, who insisted that you had to be absolutely straight with the audience, was at first uncomfortable with Oktyabrev's frivolity, but in time we persuaded him to go along with it. What finally convinced him was the argument that Pylayev's programs belonged on the same plane as the postwar political cabarets that Boris admired so much for keeping Berliners' spirits alive during the Soviet blockade of their city mounted in 1948. In fact, the Berlin radio, RIAS, where Boris had been political advisor, delighted East German audiences with a witty radio cabaret called "Die Insulaner," whose name poked fun at the Soviet blockade that had made an island of Berlin.

That first encounter of mine with Pylayev has stayed in memory for more than four decades. We Americans in postwar Germany were accustomed to being treated with the deference due to conquerors (whether we wanted it or not), not to being dressed down by a DP–though when I knew Pylayev better, I realized that the angry bluster was carefully simulated to overwhelm criticism. Inside he was laughing at me.

Pylayev was not the only émigré employee who talked back to the American *nachal'stvo*. Not long after I arrived in Munich, I had my ears pinned back by a tough little woman named Wanda Pampuch.

Wanda was the daughter of a prominent Polish Communist named Bronsky. Both of her parents had died in Stalin's purges. Wanda served seven years as a political prisoner in a gulag camp in Kolyma in the Soviet Far East, where the inmates worked at mining gold under extremely harsh conditions of intense cold and privation. On her release she returned to Moscow, where her German husband was waiting for her. They made their way to East Germany, then defected to West Berlin where she met Boris Shub, who was impressed by her political knowledge, journalistic skills, and biting wit. Through Shub's influence she was given a job at the new radio station in Munich and arrived in fall 1952 with her husband and two small children who had been born since her release. Wanda looked like a typical Communist *apparatchik*. Her pageboy haircut reminded my wife and me of Anna Pauker, the crusty Communist ruler of Romania. Inside, she had a generous heart and a wonderful sense of humor.

Wanda's husband was unemployed. Her job at RL was in those difficult times all that stood between her family and starvation. From her conduct, you would never have known it.

Ronalds and I were Wanda's supervisors. One day shortly after her arrival at RL, she came into my office. In my casual American way, I was reading with my feet propped on the desk. I looked up and found Wanda glaring at me icily. There was no humor in her stare this time.

"What's the trouble?" I asked.

"Listen," she said. "If you have your feet on the desk when I come in here the next time, you'll never see me in this place again. Even we underlings are entitled to decent human respect."

As for Pylayev, he became a familiar figure in the corridors of RL and above all in the canteen, a one-story annex that was added later. With his peasant witticisms, ginger cowlick, and knowing grin, he was the Russian village youth on the prowl in the big city. He had a peculiar swaggering, foot-slapping duckwalk that was accentuated by his habit of wearing giant loose-fitting, light-colored sandals over feet that had been savaged by winters in the gulag.

Pylayev was a master of *maternyi yazyk* (maternal language), the core of Russian obscenities that derives its name from its imaginative variations on a single theme, the concept of "motherfucker." Among our hardened veterans of Soviet reality, "maternal language" was standard, and we Americans who dealt with the employees in Russian quickly absorbed it, at least passively. Such expressions do not appear in standard dictionaries. In the United States I have known people with advanced degrees in Slavic studies who were unfamiliar with most of them.

Although respectable Russian ladies made a show of objecting to his language, Pylayev was enormously successful with women of all nationalities. I never quite understood this. Once when he and I were on the town in Munich I found myself sitting next to a beautiful young German woman who was staring at him adoringly. "What do you see in him?" I asked. "Er sieht aber so schön brutal aus" (He looks so wonderfully brutal), she replied.

He had a troubled relationship with a wife whom I do not recall ever meeting. Yet years later, when she became terminally ill, I heard that he had given up all else to be her full-time companion and devoted nurse. Pylayev was a strange compound of cynicism and sentimentality.

I had a chance to see Pylayev's charisma at work on his fellow Russians a few months after RL went on the air. After the war, former Soviet coal miners stranded in the West had found jobs in Belgian coal mines. Someone decided that we should broadcast interviews with them. I was assigned to the job and took along Pylayev, who had boasted about his contacts in the Russian community in Belgium and said he could organize the interviews in advance.

"Leave it to me," he told me, "I have a plan."

When we stepped off the night train in Brussels after a rather alcoholic journey from Munich, I asked Pylayev what preparations he had made.

"Don't get upset," he said, "I'm working on it."

It quickly became apparent that he had done nothing. While I was brooding over this discovery, he found a slip of paper in his pocket.

"Call this number," he told me, "and get Puriks on the line." (Pylayev spoke no French.)

The man named Puriks proved to be the local representative of SBONR, a postwar organization of former Soviet prisoners of war. (The letters stood for League of Struggle for the Liberation of the Peoples of Russia.) When we met him in a cafe, he agreed to Pylayev's request to send postcards right away to notify his members in the coal-mining districts of Mons and Charleroi that we were in Brussels.

Pylayev and Puriks devised a message for the cards asking the recipient to come to our hotel at 9 A.M. Sunday, two days away, and gave the number of my room. The cards included a promise that Leonid Pylayev would perform. Puriks assured us that in a small, efficient country like Belgium, next-day delivery was certain.

"What if nobody shows up?" I asked Pylayev. I had visions of returning to Munich empty-handed, my career at RL severely damaged.

"Don't worry," he reassured me haughtily. "Just order another drink, then we'll go sightseeing."

The next two days were for me an agony of apprehension of failure on this, my first important mission outside Munich. Pylayev was an enthusiastic tourist, but critical. He snorted at the Mannequin-pisse, the fountain off the Grand' Place that consists of a little boy urinating. "Chudaki, eti bel'giytsy" (Weirdos, these Belgians), he commented, and I realized that he had known only the public puritanism of Stalin's Russia and Hitler's Germany. He was scornful of the

Bruxellois habit of passing time in cafes. "Don't they have anything better to do?" he asked indignantly. The elaborate ritual of ordering multicourse meals in restaurants also failed to impress him. "Why so many decisions? Why not keep it simple? They'd still get enough to eat." In the evening, we went to nightclubs frequented by what polite Russians call "women of easy behavior," with me as Pylayev's interpreter. Was this why I had worked so hard on my Russian? I wondered.

When Sunday morning finally came, I was sleeping after a late night. There was a knock on the door of my room. Two men greeted me in Russian. It was just past eight. I called Pylayev's room and asked what to do with them.

"Send them in one at a time, and have the first one bring your tape recorder with him. When the others come, just tell them to wait. Tell them when we get all through the show will begin. And have lots of food and drink sent up to my room around noon."

So, while I acted as receptionist for a steady stream of newcomers, Pylayev taped interviews with each visitor. Sometime after midday the last one filed into his room, and I went along to see what was happening. Those who had been interviewed were waiting patiently next to a table covered with bottles and cold cuts.

The last interview finished, Pylayev switched off the tape recorder. "Nu, rebyata, davayte" (Okay, boys, let's go). He turned to me. "Pour some drinks. But first give me a water glass full of vodka."

For more than two hours, Pylayev performed. Monologues, jokes, poetry, songs, some of it sentimental, much of it scatological. The coal miners, enthralled, sat silently except for occasional bursts of guffaws. These were men who, living in a strange and rigorous environment, had been cut off for years from their native culture. I think they might have stayed for the rest of the evening if Pylayev had not dismissed them. They left us with warm handshakes and expressions of gratitude.

The interviews we took back re-created the world of the Russian coal miner in Belgium. In asking intelligent questions, Pylayev had forgotten his "Oktyabrev" persona and played the self-effacing questioner. We were greeted in Munich like returning heroes. I remember one detail with special pride. Several of the miners had compared Belgian safety technology unfavorably with even the notoriously dangerous conditions in Soviet mines. RL broadcast those portions of the interviews, too. So much for propaganda!

If Russia in those days had been a normal country, I am sure Pylayev would have been a famous comedian. As it was, he never learned languages well enough to have a significant career anywhere else. His English consisted of a single phrase, probably remembered from some old film: "She wants to know." He would make conversation with English speakers like my wife by repeating the phrase over and over again, with varying intonations. Somehow he managed to do it without ever seeming tedious. He acquired a certain fluency in German, no doubt from his bedroom adventures, but spoke it haltingly and with an atrocious accent.

He did play bit parts, however, in Western movies where a distinctively Russian face was needed.

From time to time, I see American television reruns of *The Journey,* an Anatole Litvak film produced after the 1956 Hungarian uprising, in which Yul Brynner plays a menacing Soviet officer whose unit has detained a group, among them a woman played by Deborah Kerr, trying to flee the country. Pylayev, as Brynner's adjutant, has some nice bits of business, including tricks on horseback and a Russian drinking scene.

Pylayev played a part in another film, shot in Wiesbaden and starring one of the Gabor sisters. For his work, he received 2,000 Deutschemark, then an unheard-of sum for a DP to possess. He spent the entire amount immediately, on a party at Wiesbaden's most elegant hostelry, the Nassauer Hof, to which he invited Miss Gabor (was it Zsa Zsa or Eva?) and the rest of the cast.

In the early 1950s DPs at RL earned between 400 and 500 Deutschemark a month, around $100. In this respect, there was little difference between a laborer and a former professor or engineer who might be employed in a professional capacity. The reason given was that more generous pay would "destabilize" the West German economy. At the same time, an American secretary, or an émigré hired in the United States, Britain, or France, earned four or more times as much and received free housing, deepening the social gulf between them and the DPs. (Years later at RFE/RL, the organization created in the early 1970s by the merger of Radio Liberty and Radio Free Europe, children and grandchildren of those same DPs who were employed there earned twenty to forty times as much and could be seen after work driving off in BMWs and Porsches.)

One of my most vivid memories of those early days involved an incident that flared up over freelance fees for local scriptwriters. Ronalds and I were building up a backlog of scripts for use after the station went on the air. We had decided, after some soul searching, that 40 Deutschemark per script, about $10, would be a fair amount. We would have liked to pay more. Some of the freelancers had children to support and no other hope of employment. At 40 Deutschemark, the return from one or two scripts a month was hardly enough to support a family.

We were required to send each request for a freelance payment to the American director of administration for individual approval. In the fall of 1952 the incumbent of that office, an amiable gentleman named Newton Randolph (known to one and all as Randy), was replaced by a new director sent over from the United States, a man with an imposing moniker whom I'll call here R. Davidson Swank. We quickly understood that he was one of "the boys" mentioned in the last chapter. Our first awareness of Swank in action was a pile of our payment requests sent back from his office, the usual "DM40" crossed out and "DM35" written in instead.

Thinking of our underpaid émigré colleagues, Ronalds went storming up to Swank's office with me at his heels and insubordinately demanded an explanation.

"Well," that gentleman told us complacently, "I figured if you can get something for 40 Deutschemark, there's no reason you can't get it for 35."

Something snapped in Ronalds. He reached across Swank's desk and grabbed him by the lapels. The startled man gave in, promising to restore the 40 Deutschemark payment.

Swank, perhaps inspired by the Jim Crow system that still prevailed in the American South, also proposed installing separate toilets for Soviet émigrés. On that he was overruled and left Munich and RL not long after, little mourned by those he left behind. As with so many other ephemeral American executives who came and went in those early Munich days, I have no inkling of his subsequent destiny.

The trip to Belgium formed a bond of friendship between Pylayev and me that lasted long after I left Munich nearly ten years later.

Pylayev added to my knowledge of Russian drinking habits. The cardinal rule was never to drink *bez zakuski,* without a food chaser. One employee of the Russian desk, a notorious drunk who frequently appeared at work in a helpless state of inebriation and was eventually fired for his habit, prided himself on never touching a drop without having something to eat with it. One early morning Pylayev appeared at our apartment during a visit from my mother, who had come over from New York state. For years afterward she talked about the Russian she met who for breakfast drained a tumbler full of vodka at one gulp, then wolfed down a thick slice of raw onion on a piece of rye bread.

Given the hard-drinking milieu in which he had existed, Pylayev imbibed relatively moderately. Often in the morning, when tables in the canteen were covered with large half-liter glasses of beer being enjoyed by other staff members as their first drink of the day, Pylayev could be seen with a beer glass filled with milk. Only later in the day would he switch to vodka. One habit in particular marked his drinking: he insisted that he could drink vodka only in a certain way, by downing at one gulp 200 grams (more than 6 ounces), never a smaller dose. The usual custom was for a group of drinkers to drink bottoms-up in unison from small glasses, a process punctuated by toasts. Instead of drinking each toast, Pylayev would pour his shot of vodka into a large glass. When finally the glass was full, he would empty it in one swallow that brought tears to his eyes and made him choke, to the acclaim and merriment of his fellow drinkers, who by that time were ready to find his every action hilarious. With Pylayev, one never knew whether such habits were genuine or a pose designed to enhance his theatrical image.

My friendship with him was not always serene, though, because of my role in the *nachal'stvo*.

Toward the end of my Munich stay I was given overall responsibility for Russian broadcasts (of which more later). My predecessor, a generous man, had in the meantime elevated Pylayev from freelance contributor to permanent salaried status on the regular staff of the Russian desk. The result, which any of Pylayev's friends could have predicted, was a drastic fall in his output, depriving both the station and the Soviet audience of his regular talks. When I came into the picture, the solution was obvious: friend or no friend, Pylayev had to go back on freelance status. If we paid him enough per script, he could actually earn more, and everyone would be better off, all the way to Kamchatka.

To fire Pylayev I first had to secure approval from RL's general counsel, a little gnome of a Viennese-American refugee named Paul Moeller, who enjoyed a reputation for shrewdness. When I outlined the circumstances, including Pylayev's low productivity, Moeller told me flatly, "Fire him. He doesn't have a leg to stand on." Next day I called in Pylayev.

"Well, Lyonya," I told him, "this is it. We're firing you." Then I outlined my plan to reward him for freelance contributions. Pylayev eyed me with a distant gleam. "We'll see," he said.

Next day I heard through the Oberwiesenfeld grapevine that Pylayev had come in to see General Counsel Moeller, bringing a German lawyer with him. In short order my phone rang. It was Moeller.

"About this fellow Pylayev. You'll have to cancel his dismissal and take him back."

"But you said he didn't have a leg to stand on."

"I know. But you've got to hire him back. His lawyer convinced me."

I gave in, but not for long. A few weeks later Pylayev was absent from the office for such a long period that I was sure I could terminate him for cause. I talked again with Moeller. "Okay, this time you've got him," he said. "Let him go." He repeated a familiar phrase: "He doesn't have a leg to stand on."

The next day, as before, I heard that Pylayev was in with his lawyer, and Moeller called me again. "I guess you'll have to keep him."

I tried one more time to get Pylayev off the salary rolls, for some particularly egregious violation of discipline. Once again the pattern was repeated, with Moeller telling me he "doesn't have a leg to stand on" and then calling to tell me to keep him.

I gave up.

During all these incidents, Pylayev and I never stopped socializing with each other. Usually we met with a group for drinks after work. There was never the least sign of personal rancor on his part. I was just doing my job as one of the infamous *nachal'stvo*.

Pylayev did get revenge of a kind on me, and also on Ronalds, who had participated in my attempt to deprive him of his salaried job. The opportunity was a sweet one for him.

After working late one evening, Ronalds and I were sitting over a drink in a rather upscale *Gaststätte,* eating and drinking establishment, when we discovered that between us we lacked the funds to pay the tab. As if by a miracle, in walked an elegant Leonid Pylayev, resplendent in a tuxedo and with his ginger cowlick slicked down. (This was during one of his movie jobs.)

We threw ourselves at him, begging for a loan of 10 marks. Pylayev turned to the waiter and said, "These men are bothering me. I refuse to stay in this place." He spun on his heel and left. Ronalds and I, hostages to the *Gaststätte,* had to stay behind. Finally, in des-

peration, we called someone—one of our wives, as I recall—and persuaded her to bring us money to bail us out.

One day Pylayev avenged himself on me in another way. There
was a running chess tournament in the canteen, the stakes a standard
one Deutschemark per game. It always struck me as ironic that while
we Americans played pinball at lunchtime, if we ate in the canteen at
all, the much lower-paid ex-Soviets were hunched over their chess-
boards. When in 1957 the Soviet Union launched the first Sputnik, I
was less surprised than some other Americans.

Along with his other talents, Pylayev was a formidable chess
player. In the canteen, when not entertaining, he could usually be
seen at the chessboard. Only one other RL employee could match
him, a fussy little old Russian desk staffer in gold-rimmed pince-nez
named Kul'bitsky. It was Kul'bitsky's hallmark never to appear on the
premises without a necktie and starched collar. When the usually slov-
enly Pylayev played Kul'bitsky, a crowd always gathered to watch.

Once I walked into the canteen just as Pylayev and Kul'bitsky
were finishing their latest contest. Pylayev looked up at me from the
board. "Let's have a game," he said with a grin. Normally I would
have declined, but for some reason on that day I accepted. Predictably, Pylayev beat me in three quick games. I handed over my three
marks and called a halt to the slaughter.

"Playing with you is an expensive pleasure," I said.

He looked at me contemptuously. "Put it this way. I'm doing you
a favor. If you were paying me to give you lessons it would be a lot
more expensive."

The exchange was witnessed and enjoyed by several other employees who never dared speak to an American so caustically and
who relished seeing me embarrassed by Pylayev's audacity.

Pylayev's influence on the rank and file even affected the way
they spoke Russian. If he called someone a *dunduk,* an unflattering
name for "jerk" that is not in many dictionaries, I would hear people
using the word all over the station for the next few weeks.

In his perverse way Pylayev taught us, as did other employees in
different ways, to respect the new émigrés and through them to ex-
tend the same respect to our silent and unseen listeners in the Soviet
Union.

That was an important lesson in an age of manipulation, of "psychological warfare," when books were being written with such titles as
Strategic Psychological Operations and American Foreign Policy or *Techniques*

of Persuasion. Years later, when the Soviet Union began to open up, we discovered that RL's attitude of respect was an essential ingredient in establishing its relationship of trust with its audiences.

People like Wladimir Weidle and Victor Frank were the brains of Radio Liberty. Pylayev, for all his crudity, was its soul.

Country Boy
in Germany

4

How did a boy like me from rural Dutchess County, New York, become mixed up with political broadcasts to the Soviet Union, rubbing shoulders with Russians, Ukrainians, Uzbeks, Tatars, Armenians—a whole exotic mix of nationalities, many of them considered "enemies of the people" by the Kremlin, a few accused of being war criminals, some suspected (by our side) of being KGB plants?

The short answer is that I became bored by my work as an advertising copywriter with the General Electric Company in Schenectady, went back to school to study Russian (with help from the GI Bill and my wife Pat's salary as a government personnel assistant), and was offered the job in Munich by a casual acquaintance.

The longer answer is that I had been groping for broader horizons ever since my lonely childhood on the farm where, aside from my sister Joan, two years younger, there were no other children to play with. My parents encouraged me to read and I did, voraciously, partly as an escape from tending cows and chickens. My father had been a teacher before going into the college textbook business, and he had me learning Latin by the time I was ten. My mother started me on French and German at an even earlier age; she had been in England and France during World War I as secretary to the commanding officer of a U.S. Army hospital and had then gone off to Turkey and the Caucasus with the Near East Relief Society. On weekends, especially during the summer months, our house came alive with visitors from New York City, two hours away, and other more distant points. I was used to being under the same roof with British, French, German, and Russian friends of my parents and to hearing discussions about which restaurants were best in Constantinople or Vienna. I used to lie in bed at night, listening to the ripple

of the brook, the owls in our apple orchard, and the lonely whistle
of a locomotive on the Harlem Valley line a few miles away, and
dream of growing up and getting away from that setting, which
others found idyllic but which to me seemed dull and confining.
I longed for a world of adventure and drama.

During the week and on winter weekends when there were no
house guests, I would relieve the tedium by pasting stamps from
faraway places into my album or listening to foreign stations on the
Silvertone shortwave radio that my parents bought in 1936. I have a
vivid memory from 1940 of a bemused and baffled broadcast from
Berlin by the British humorist P. G. Wodehouse soon after advancing
German troops had captured him at his French home. Also from Berlin, I can still hear the mocking tones of "Lord Haw Haw," the traitor
William Joyce who was hanged by the British at war's end. There was
also the pro-Fascist American poet Ezra Pound broadcasting from
Rome, "Paris Mondial," until the Germans occupied that city, and on
one memorable occasion a faint English voice from Moscow, the city
then being threatened by German invaders. My staple, though, was
the overseas service of the BBC; as the Battle of Britain dragged on,
my parents began to clamor for BBC broadcasts, too, making me feel
important as I tuned expertly over the dial.

In Dover Plains, the nearest town, three miles away, I became involved with a group who were interested in amateur radio, a natural
outgrowth of my exposure to shortwave. By the age of thirteen, I
had arisen early one morning to take two trains by myself to get to
Schenectady, where I passed the Federal Communications Commission code and theory exams for a "Class B" amateur license on the
first try, then returned by two more trains to the farm on the same
day. The heady experience of having my own call letters, W2NKE,
led me to miscalculate my whole future. I now realize that my interest
in radio related mostly to its purely communication aspects; at the
time I thought I was destined to become a great electronics engineer.

My father had wanted me to go to Yale, his alma mater. To his
chagrin, I insisted on enrolling instead at the Massachusetts Institute
of Technology. The most important thing I learned at MIT, but was
too stubborn to admit to my parents, was my lack of the passion for
pieces of inanimate equipment needed to be able to enjoy long,
lonely hours crouched over a laboratory bench. The last years of
World War II brought that lesson home further when my college

career was interrupted by service as a naval airborne radar technician, handling more pieces of inanimate equipment.

With degree in hand in 1948, I turned down offers of employment as an engineer and accepted a job in General Electric's advertising and sales promotion divisions as a copywriter trainee. At least that brought me into contact with people who were interested in language and communication, but trying to generate rhapsodic prose about things like large motors and generators left me feeling unfulfilled. I married Patricia Coe, a Wellesley graduate whom I had met on a blind date when we were still students. Pat and I set up housekeeping in Schenectady, a company town where we soon began to feel the walls closing in on us. Still, for lack of a suitable alternative we might have stayed there to raise our family. It was the Cold War that liberated us.

Pat and I used to spend weekends at the farm of my boyhood, where my widowed mother was living. One September Sunday morning in 1950, while I lay sleeping, Pat and my mother had driven into Dover Plains for the *New York Times*. By the time I woke up my future had been decided: they had discovered an article in the paper about the pressing U.S. need for people to study Russian so as to cope with the new Soviet challenge. The article listed a half-dozen universities, then the only ones in the nation offering Russian-language studies.

Back in Schenectady on Monday morning, I called in sick and stayed home to telephone the universities on the list. Several told me that it was too late in the year to accept my application. Finally, I called Georgetown University's newly formed Institute of Languages and Linguistics in Washington, D.C., which proved to be desperate for students. The director, Leon Dostert, accepted me on the telephone on the basis only of my oral assurance that I had some kind of degree from somewhere.

At Georgetown I plunged into a program of total immersion in Russian, leavened only by a few other courses. The language instructors, it turned out, were all members of the NTS, an organization of Russian nationalists that passed for the best organized and most "revolutionary" of the émigré political groups. We became friends, and I began to spend many extracurricular hours with them. This was an association of mutual advantage: it gave me a chance to perfect my Russian conversation, and them the opportunity to exploit my English-language skills, getting me to grind out material promoting the NTS for potential American supporters. The NTS program was simple: give us some help and we'll get the Russian people to overthrow their hated Communist oppressors. I thought it sounded like a good idea and was eager to assist. Later, I began to meet people around Washington who convinced me that the reality was not quite that simple. But I am indebted to the NTS for making me quite fluent in Russian in only one year, qualifying me for a job with the director of intelligence of the Atomic Energy Commission (AEC).

One person who expressed skepticism to me about the NTS was Guy Burgess, the British Embassy secretary now known to have been a Soviet spy. Burgess spent an afternoon in our apartment under rather peculiar circumstances. A friend, a former fellow student at Georgetown, had met him on a boat coming from Europe and was fascinated by his conversation but put off by Burgess's obvious interest in pursuing a sexual relationship. The friend asked whether he could bring Burgess to our apartment as neutral ground where he would feel safe from unwelcome advances. Pat and I agreed, and one rather chilly January afternoon in 1952 the two showed up in Burgess's open touring car. We were struck by his appearance: his Eton tie knotted around the collar of a greenish plaid lumberjack shirt surmounted by a fluffy pink jacket, and his constant habit of scratching himself in private places.

In hindsight, knowing that Burgess had by then been tipped off that he was under suspicion as a Soviet agent, I think he must have suspected me of connections with U.S. intelligence, because this man with a bibulous reputation steadfastly refused to accept a drink, instead pulling a silver flask of his own from a hip pocket from time to time.

Burgess was a raconteur. He told us with relish a story of having gone down to Churchill's estate in 1938, on the day after the Munich Pact was signed dooming Czechoslovakia to German encroachment. "To console the old man," as he put it. He said he found Churchill puttering around the garden.

"Ah, Mr. Burgess, good of you to come," Churchill supposedly told him, fishing in his pocket and handing Burgess a tattered piece of paper. It was a telegram from Eduard Beneš, the Czechoslovak president, asking for Churchill's intercession with the British government.

"I've had this from Herr Beans," Burgess said Churchill told him, as he mimicked the Churchillian pronunciation of the Czech's name. "What can I tell him, Mr. Burgess, what can I tell him?" Telling us the story, Burgess said that, for want of anything better, he had murmured some banalities in reply.

I wondered at the time why Burgess, who seemed to have no particular personal or political relationship with Churchill, would have paid this call. Once again, in hindsight, I now wonder whether he had not been sent by his bosses in Moscow to find out how an important British politician was reacting to the news of Munich.

I maneuvered the conversation around to the Soviet Union, which Burgess seemed somehow reluctant to discuss. Today I blush at the thought of how the veteran Soviet agent must have been laughing inwardly as I naively recited to him the NTS formula for saving Russia.

At some point during the discussion, Mao Zedong was mentioned. Burgess, who had picked up a drawing pad from the table next to him, began to do page after page of Mao caricatures. Afterward we threw them out. If we had kept them, would they have been collector's items today?

Toward the end of his visit, Burgess went through our phonograph records and pulled Offenbach's *Gaieté Parisienne* from the stack. He played it over and over at top volume, making the dishes rattle and the walls tremble, probably (I now think) a ploy to deafen any FBI agents who might be bugging our conversation. When a few months later we heard on the radio that he had disappeared, presumably to defect to the Soviet Union, we worried that we might be in trouble at the AEC—where both of us were then employed with top-secret "Q" clearances—because Burgess might have left behind the notebook in which he had jotted down our address. The security people at AEC told us not to worry: Burgess had so many Washington friends in high places that our minor brush with him would hardly attract attention.

I was restless at the AEC—too much technology again—and began to look for a way out. Among the Washington people I had met while I was a student at Georgetown was a State Department official named Manning H. Williams, who had given me occasional freelance translations to do for his office. One day in 1952 Manning called to tell me he was leaving the State Department to go to Munich and set up a radio station. He asked whether I would care to join the staff. Did my boyhood dreams of broader horizons play a role in my answer? Probably. In any case, I rejoiced at the chance, and before long Pat and I were checking into the Regina-Palast Hotel in Munich as residents.

I went to Munich on a short-term contract, expecting to stay for one year. In the end I remained at Radio Liberty for twenty years before leaving to join the U.S. Information Agency. Why did I stay so long? Perhaps because I'm one of those people who have to choke back tears of joy when the good guys triumph in a movie. I've seen *Casablanca* dozens of times, but I do it all over again when the French patriots stand up in Rick's nightclub and sing "La Marseillaise" to drown out the German officers with their "Wacht am Rhein." Boris Shub taught me to guard against that corny side of my nature in my work at RL, but it's still there deep down. I knew that for sure when the Soviet Union collapsed.

Moscow
Strikes Back

5

The Kremlin response to Radio Liberation's debut was not long in coming. It took various forms, all of them sobering, some sinister.

In terms of day-to-day activity at the station, the direst Soviet counter-action was violence, or the threat of violence. RL employees, especially the émigrés, had good cause to fear each day for their lives.

In 1954, the year after RL went on the air, the head of the Azerbaijani desk, a short, dark, intense man named Abdul Fatalibey, failed to show up for work one morning. Fatalibey's background was like that of so many other RL employees: service in the Red Army, capture by the Germans followed by service in a German-organized unit, escape at war's end from the Allied repatriation action, then life in occupied Germany as a displaced person. Whether from birth or experience, he wore a permanent expression of bitterness and disillusionment.

When after a few days Fatalibey had still not appeared, the Bavarian police began a search. What followed was tragic, but with overtones of farce. The police eventually discovered a body in the apartment of another Azerbaijani, one Ismailov. The body had been bound with wire and mutilated. Attached to it was a sign containing a warning to "traitors to the motherland." The police reasoned that the body belonged to Ismailov and that our missing colleague Fatalibey must be the murderer. According to this theory, Fatalibey was probably an undercover agent of the Soviets.

It was only after a couple of weeks that friends of Fatalibey, who insisted on his innocence, were able to persuade the police to take a closer look at the body. It was duly exhumed and, to much official embarrassment, proved to be that of RL's missing Azerbaijani desk chief. Now suspicion swung to the tenant of the apartment, who until then had been thought to be dead. His guilt, and the involvement of the

Soviet secret police in Fatalibey's murder, seemed to be established beyond a doubt when later on he was reported to be in East Germany.

A second death occurred not long after Fatalibey's. The body of an employee of the Belorussian desk was found in the Isar River. There was no evidence of foul play, but the victim was known to be a man of good habits, with no record of despondency or suicidal tendencies. Exactly how he died never came to light, but we, and the authorities, thought it likely that the Soviets were behind this incident as well.

As far as we knew, only those two RL employees were killed by the Soviets, but other operations by KGB assassins in West Germany helped to maintain an atmosphere of dread at the station. In 1954 an agent named Nikolai Khokhlov, using a phony Swiss passport (one of the most difficult in the world to counterfeit), arrived in Frankfurt with orders to kill a leader of the NTS organization of Russian nationalists, a man named Georgii Okolovich. Khokhlov had a change of heart. Instead of killing Okolovich, he sought him out and confessed his true identity. Tipped off in advance by the CIA, I covered the Frankfurt press conference at which the Khokhlov case was "surfaced," and I will never forget how the rows of journalists ducked when a munitions expert pointed at us the bullet-firing cigarette case with which Khokhlov had been armed.

The Khokhlov story of secret weapons and sudden remorse was so fantastic that it aroused suspicion in some quarters; skeptical journalists wondered whether it had been concocted by zealots at the CIA to discredit the Soviets. The story gained credibility, however, when the Russian-born wife of Associated Press journalist Thomas Whitney announced that she remembered Khokhlov from Moscow, where she had been a concert artist under her maiden name of Yulia Zampol'skaia. Khokhlov had moved in her circle. Later on, Khokhlov gained further credibility when doctors discovered an attempt to poison him, to which the KGB later owned up. He wound up at an American university.

Just before his press conference, Khokhlov gave me an interview for RL in which he described his various missions for the KGB and the reasons, political and personal, for his decision not to fulfill the latest one. What I remember best, though, was a trivial exchange with the erstwhile KGB operative while we were chatting after the interview had been taped. The Soviet government had recently announced, with much fanfare, that it was beginning mass production of champagne, "Sovetskoye shampanskoye." Knowing that Khokhlov's undercover assignments for the KGB had taken him to France, I asked him a question: "You're one of the few people who've had the opportunity to compare Soviet and French champagne—which one tastes better?" This was not long after Stalin's death, when travel to and from the Soviet Union was still a rarity.

"Oh," Khokhlov replied, "I like Soviet champagne better."

"Why?" I asked in astonishment.

"It tastes more like champagne, you know."

Later on, when I was living in France, I could dine out on the story of Khokhlov's comparison of French and Soviet champagne; my French friends reacted with universal horror and indignation. Still later, on visits to areas of the Soviet Union where drinking water was unsafe and sickly sweet Soviet champagne was one of the few available alternatives, I used to remember Khokhlov's reply with consternation.

In 1957 and 1959 a Soviet agent named Bohdan Stashynsky, who was equipped by Moscow with special tubes that fired poison pellets, committed two concealed murders, both in Munich. His victims were prominent Ukrainian émigrés, Lev Rebet and Stefan Bandera. In Rebet's case, the cause of death was diagnosed as heart failure. In Bandera's case, an autopsy revealed traces of prussic acid. KGB involvement in both deaths became certain when in 1961 Stashynsky, who meanwhile had been decorated in Moscow, fled to the West with his East German girlfriend, asked for political asylum, and confessed details of both crimes. He was sentenced to a prison term.

Another facet of the terror campaign against RL was the night visitors who would ring an émigré employee's doorbell. When the employee responded, a stranger would be standing on the doorstep, holding up a photo of a parent, spouse, or child who was still in the Soviet Union. "You'd better let me in," the stranger would say.

The stranger would usually hand the émigré a letter from some close relative back home, begging him or her to return. The visitor might then offer to help his involuntary host or hostess make arrangements to return to the Soviet Union. Such arrangements were easy to make: in East Berlin there was a Soviet "Committee for Return to the Homeland," headed at one point by an army major-general. The committee had its own radio broadcasts and a newspaper that it mailed to our employees' homes. When someone moved, the committee caught up with the change of address with eerie efficiency, a reminder that the KGB or someone had good sources inside our organization.

The people used for "night visitor" assignments were most often Germans from the Soviet-controlled part of the country; some were paid *Vertrauensleute* (agents of confidence), while others were black-mailed into cooperation through threats to their own relatives. Because they were committing no actual crime, it was difficult to prevent their harassment of our émigré employees.

Given the climate of assassination, appearance of a mysterious stranger at an émigré's door was terrifying enough. Just as terrifying was the target's realization that the KGB had approached his or her relatives and coerced or cajoled them—one could only imagine by what means—to cooperate in persuading the émigré to return. There was always the implied threat that, if the employee did not comply, something horrible might happen to loved ones.

Often, the employee would come to work next morning and head for the RL security officer to tell him what had happened. We also learned of cases where fear had kept people from reporting the visits. In still other instances, the Soviet campaign succeeded.

Our first "redefector" was a female announcer named Oliynyk-Upitis; after all these years I think her first name was Halyna, but I am not sure. Although an ethnic Ukrainian, she voiced Russian pro-grams for RL. We had no inkling that she was unhappy with her work at RL. One day, the Soviet media startled us with an announcement that she had returned voluntarily to her homeland.

The Soviet press attributed several hostile statements about RL to Oliynyk-Upitis. In one of them, she supposedly accused me of being a "supplier of false witnesses." This baffled me until a later story quoted her as referring to a certain Soviet citizen of Greek origin named Georgiadis who had visited the station after one of the post-Stalin amnesties led to his release from the gulag and permission to leave the country.

I had made arrangements for Georgiadis to spend a few days in Munich on his way to a new home in Greece. He showed up at the airport, a spry old man with irrepressible high spirits in spite of the hardships he had endured. He was dressed in leggings and a Russian fur hat and carried a crooked walking stick that was his constant com-panion. During his brief stay in Munich, he made a vivid impression on the RL staff, regaling us with stories of life in the prison camp at Vorkuta above the Arctic Circle. Because I had seen newspaper pho-tographs of Georgiadis's arrival at Stockholm Airport on a flight from the Soviet Union, I never understood the allegation that he was a "false witness"—that is, someone whom we in the West had supposedly equipped with a phony Soviet past.

Not long after the Oliynyk-Upitis incident, another one of our Russian announcers returned to the Soviet Union. Boris Vinogradov was a handsome, likable man with a dapper mustache, a wonderfully rich radio voice, and a bit of a drinking problem. I regarded him as a friend, and he never gave me occasion to regret it. He made no secret of his desire to return to his beloved Leningrad and resume his acting career, which had been cut short by the war.

"What future is there in the West for a Russian actor?" he used to ask me.

Vinogradov was one of the first émigrés at RL to acquire a car. He left for Leningrad at the wheel of his Volkswagen Beetle with a woman friend, a beautiful German redhead named Sonya Sachs who spoke perfect Russian, sitting beside him. Afterward, some of his friends at RL speculated that it was Sonya who had persuaded him to take the step. In any case, I was pleased to learn some years later that—unlike some of the returnees—he had not been imprisoned but had been given an apartment in Leningrad and allowed to keep his VW. I hope that he was also allowed to be an actor again, but if so he never became famous. The Soviets circulated a picture of Vinogradov posing in Leningrad beside his Volkswagen as an inducement to other émigrés to follow in his footsteps, which may explain their lenient treatment of him.

In one other case, we actually connived with an émigré to help him return to the Soviet Union. A kindly elderly man named Epishev worked in the monitoring section, which was then one of my responsibilities. A former military officer for whom personal honor was as important as life itself, he willingly and diligently performed the menial task of operating the mimeograph machine. He was educated, well spoken, and extremely reliable. He asked to see me one day and came into the office.

"Mr. Critchlow, you've always treated me well, and now I want to play fair with you."

"What is it, Vasilii Pavlovich?"

"My wife and I have no love for the Soviet system, but we've decided we want to be buried in Russian soil. So I'm going to get in touch with the Soviet authorities in Bonn and ask them to let us come home. I suppose you'll want me to stop working at the radio right away—you can have my resignation."

I asked Epishev to hold off on his resignation until I could speak to the security officer, at that time a young man named Jim Condon who, unlike many others who held that job, was gifted with great human understanding and compassion. I explained the facts to Jim, who readily agreed that we could let Epishev keep on working.

A few weeks later, Epishev came to my office again.

"Well," he told me, "it's all set. We leave in a few days."

I wished him well.

"There's just one thing," Epishev added. "I know that system well. The minute they get their hands on me, I'll cease to be my own master. They'll undoubtedly make me say terrible things about the radio, maybe even about you personally. I just want you to know in advance that none of it will be true."

It came to pass exactly as Epishev had said it would. After his return, Soviet media quoted him as calling RL "a dirty mouthpiece." He included me in a list of "American agents."

I hope that he and his wife are resting peacefully, and that their final years were not too troubled.

My name also figured prominently in the case of two other RL returnees to the Soviet Union. Both had defected in early 1956, one as a young senior lieutenant in the Soviet Army, the other as a bear trainer with the Moscow circus. The officer, Ivan Vasilevich Ovchinnikov, had been assigned to help with communications at a four-power conference in Berlin. He walked over to the Western side—this was before the wall was built—and requested political asylum. The bear trainer, a young man named Il'yinsky whose first name escapes me (later on the Soviet press gave his initials as I. S.), had jumped off a train taking his circus to Belgium while it was passing through West Germany.

I became acquainted with each man not long after his arrival in the West. The U.S. government had given me permission to visit its Defector Reception Center near Frankfurt, and interviewing new émigrés from the Soviet Union became a regular part of my duties at RL. In likely cases, I would also arrange for the person to come to Munich for employment interviews.

Lieutenant Ovchinnikov, a bright young man who had learned French and Romanian at a Moscow institute, quickly obtained a job on the news desk. Later, he transferred to the Russian desk, where he stood out because of his frequent complaints that the broadcasts were insufficiently "anti-Communist." He was an austere person, socially a bit of a recluse.

Unlike Ovchinnikov, bear trainer Il'yinsky was an open-faced, warm, and outgoing person who easily made friends at RL. Because radio stations have little need for bear trainers as such, he was assigned to the monitoring section where he transcribed Soviet radio broadcasts. I think Il'yinsky missed his bears. He deplored the way they had been treated by the circus. During our first conversation, he launched into a long jeremiad on the subject, indicating that his defection had been motivated in large part by his unwillingness to be a party to abuse of the animals.

"Oh, those poor bears," Il'yinsky would moan after a few drinks. "Those poor bears."

One day in November 1958 we noticed that both Ovchinnikov and Il'yinsky were missing from work. In view of the KGB's campaign against RL employees, such absences were always a matter of concern, but no one was prepared for the news that broke in a few days. Both men surfaced on November 18 in East Berlin at a press conference held under the auspices of the Soviet Embassy, at which they declared their intention to return to the Soviet Union. They spoke harshly of RL and the time they had spent there. What I remember best, for personal reasons, was their declaration at the press conference that I was a *razvedchik* (intelligence operative), a statement that was duly reported the next day in *Pravda* and *Izvestiya*.

Were these simply homesick young men who felt they had made a mistake in fleeing to the West? Were they Soviet "plants" all along? We never knew the answer. The hunch among the émigrés was that, if either was a plant, it was Ovchinnikov, and that the mild-mannered, easygoing bear trainer had fallen under his influence. They were a most unlikely twosome.

I never again heard news of the bear trainer, but in Ovchinnikov's case there was an epilogue. Years later a document appeared in *samizdat,* the Soviet dissidents' clandestine distribution network. It was written by Vladimir Osipov, leader of a conservative, religiously oriented Russian dissident faction. He reported that Ovchinnikov, after serving a term in the camps, had joined his circle, but he expressed doubt about the latter's bona fides, hinting that he was a KGB informer.

Was Ovchinnikov really imprisoned after returning from the West? Or was that a fiction, designed to cover his identity as a KGB agent? Was he planted in Osipov's movement, to keep an eye on him? Did he come to the West and join RL for the same reason? The answer to these questions must lie in KGB archives—if anyone cares enough to look for it.

In one case there was little doubt that the defector was either a plant from the beginning or had become a Soviet agent while working at RL. In 1965, after I had left Munich, a certain Oleg Tumanov defected from a Soviet ship in a foreign port. He was recruited by RL some six months later. He worked at the station for twenty years, rising to be acting chief editor of the Russian service. In 1986 he returned to Moscow, where he claimed at a press conference held on April 28 of that year that the CIA was still running Radio Free Europe (RFE) and RL, although that agency's involvement had been ended more than ten years earlier with much public fanfare in Washington. Tumanov also boasted of having collected "confidential" information for the Soviets while he was an RL employee. He did not boast of his role in the February 1981 bombing of the building where he worked, which by then housed the combined RFE/RL studios. It was only after the Soviet collapse that one of his KGB bosses revealed in a book that Tumanov had had a major hand in that action, which injured four of his colleagues. At the time Soviet media charged that the blast had been engineered by U.S. intelligence in a feeble effort to gain sympathy for RFE/RL and that I was one of the perpetrators.

The possibility that among your fellow employees there might be people who were working for the KGB, perhaps reporting to potential assassins on your movements, was naturally unsettling to employee morale. Still, our émigré colleagues were a brave and stoical group who did not dwell for long on such threats. It always amazed me that people who could laugh in the face of danger were at the same time quick to make an emotional scene about seemingly trivial annoyances, such as having an editor change a word in one of their programs or being asked to work under fluorescent lights, to which people were not accustomed in postwar Germany.

Events following the KGB bombing of the RFE/RL studios in 1980, nearly two decades after I left Munich, brought home to me what close tabs the KGB had been keeping on me personally over the years. I left the New York headquarters of RL, where I worked until 1972, to join the U.S. Information Agency in Washington as head of Soviet and East European research. In that capacity I visited the Soviet Union three times, with a diplomatic passport and visa. During those visits officials gave me a normal reception, and media attacks on RL stopped mentioning my name. Then in 1976 I joined the staff of the U.S. Board for International Broadcasting, the federal oversight agency for RL and RFE, and the attacks on me resumed. In 1985, just before Mikhail Gorbachev took office as general secretary, a novel was published in Moscow in which I appeared, under my own name, as one of the characters.

The novel's author was identified as Vitalii Viktorov, a name unknown to Western specialists in Soviet literature, leading to the suspicion that it was the pseudonym for a collective KGB effort. The plot of the novel centered on the Munich bombing, a real event. The rest was sheer fantasy.

According to the scenario given in this Soviet novel, the bombing was actually a gimmick, a "provocation," staged by the CIA to win sympathy and support for RFE/RL. My job was supposedly to relay instructions from Washington to the conspirators in Munich. The personal references to me were highly unflattering. For example, I was portrayed during a clandestine meeting in the elegant Cafe Annast in Munich as pouring shots of vodka into my beer, a practice of Russian alcoholics that is viewed as highly decadent.

The novel describes a friend's reaction on meeting me after not having seen me for many years: "At the table in the cafe Richard barely recognized Critchlow. The years had done their work. Before him sat a middle-aged, gray-haired, completely fat and flabby person."

The boys in Moscow must have had fun with that one.

More chilling were references in the novel to my family. My wife Pat and daughters Ann and Jane were referred to by name, with the accurate information that our daughters were just finishing college. When I told my family that they had become characters in a Soviet novel, they were not amused that the KGB was keeping track of them.

I have never met anyone who took these Soviet charges against me seriously. In any case, I was eventually "cleared" by a former KGB general, Oleg Kalugin, who published his memoirs in English in 1994. Kalugin admitted that the bombing was his own idea and that former RL employee Oleg Tumanov had helped with the dirty work.

With the KGB a constant threat at RL, we were generally content to leave security matters to specialists in the field. Sometimes, though, the security people seemed to go off on the wrong tangent, and there was little we could do about it.

One such problem involved Wanda Pampuch, the peppery ex-Communist who warned me in 1952 never to put my feet on my desk in her presence. Despite that incident, my wife and I had developed warm and friendly relations with her, which we cemented a few weeks after the event when all of us attended a conference at Bad Homburg, some five hours' drive from Munich. A few months later, Manning Williams called Ronny Ronalds and me to his office. Choking back the tears, he told us that Wanda was being dismissed from the staff immediately and that we were to have absolutely nothing to do with her, either professionally or socially. It was unnecessary for him to explain that this was a security decision. What else could be responsible?

Many years later, it still gives me searing pain to confess that I complied with these instructions and turned my back on a friend. I never for one minute believed that Wanda was a Soviet agent or anything of the sort, although it was plausible that her independent spirit might have led her to stay in contact with personal friends on the other side and even to see them indiscreetly. But orders were orders, unless I wanted to quit RL. I remember all the rationalizations that I used to excuse my conduct. For example, if I lost my job, then I'd probably be replaced by someone who would do it less well, who might let down the other émigrés who seemed to be dependent on me at RL. The incident with Wanda was a shattering experience, one that for the rest of my life has made me slow to judge the activities of others on moral grounds.

Wanda was "clean," I know, if only because our fellow station RFE was still allowed to use her as a freelance. I tried to appeal the security decision against her on that ground, but the answer was a firm no.

While all this was going on, my wife and I ran into Wanda while she was feeding the ducks with her children in Munich's English Garden. She recognized us but looked away grimly.

Years later, when I was working for RL in New York at a higher level, and had grown more sure of myself, I heard that Wanda was in town with her son, now a young man. In the meantime, after great initial hardships, she had carved out a successful career as a West German journalist. I called her, and she agreed to pay us a visit. After a meal and some pleasant, innocuous chitchat, I broached the subject that had been troubling me nearly every day for so many years.

"Oh, that," Wanda said. "I knew exactly where you were coming from. There were plenty of people like you in the Soviet Union."

Her words were not very comforting.

Electronic jamming of our broadcasts, although less brutal in human terms than other Soviet counter-measures, was more effective in hampering our operation. Predictably, within seconds of the start of our first broadcasts, on March 1, 1953, Soviet jamming transmitters began operating on the same frequencies to blot them out. We expected this, because other radio stations, such as Voice of America and BBC, were already receiving the same treatment.

I always used to marvel at the efficiency of the Soviet jamming network. Operating over a vast space that embraced eleven time zones and one-sixth of all the land on earth, its staffs had to hear and identify "hostile" broadcasts on any frequency and in any language, then report them to a central headquarters, where someone had to issue the appropriate instructions to jamming transmitters spread all over the country. The Soviet economy might not be able to produce enough food or a decent vacuum bottle, but when it came to priorities like trying to block voices from outside, the efficiency was awesome.

For decades, until Mikhail Gorbachev and perestroika finally put an end to jamming, the jammers were right on us, always within seconds of the time that we opened up on a new frequency.

Jamming transmitters used to identify themselves with a Morse code call-signal. Someone once counted 1,800 of them. Jamming towers became a regular part of the scenery in Soviet and East European cities. When I first visited Moscow in 1973, after I had left RL, I spotted one right next to my hotel, the massive Ukraina on the Moscow River. It was a "ground wave" jammer, very effective for drowning broadcasts in densely populated areas but limited in range. To cover the space between cities, the Soviets used "sky wave" jammers, ordinary shortwave transmitters that were less effective than the "ground wave" kind because their signals were spread thinner but which were able to blanket a much larger area. In those early days both varieties of jammers merely broadcast a grating, disagreeable noise on the frequency of the offending station. Later the modulation became more sophisticated.

Long after I had left RL and several years after the collapse of the Soviet Union, I spotted a massive shortwave transmitter installation while riding a train through Mongolia, a former Soviet satellite. The antennas seemed to go on for miles and miles. Mongolia, I realized, was just the right distance to blanket densely populated western sections of the USSR with "sky wave" jamming signals because "sky waves," which are reflected from the ionosphere, skip over considerable distances before returning to earth. Ironically, in Russia itself in the post-Soviet era, the government has been obtaining revenue by leasing former jamming transmitters to capitalist advertisers, an interesting switch.

Jamming reduced the size of the audience but never eliminated it completely. It cut out the casual listeners but left us with those who were highly motivated. Some Muscovites and other city dwellers would make special weekend trips, particularly in time of crisis, to the countryside where the jamming was less effective.

Not long after we went on the air at RL, two people in the production section came down to our offices on the second floor one day and informed us breathlessly that they had devised an "antijamming technique." One was Ernst Konstantin, our chief producer, a German actor who was a native speaker of Russian; he had lived in the country as a boy while his father sold Singer sewing machines there. The other was a Russian-American producer named Vadim Gontzoff (his English spelling of the Russian "Gontsov"), who had a deep Russian bass, a powerful set of lungs, and professional voice training. We rushed up to one of the studios to see the new "technique" demonstrated and watched in awe as Gontzoff, his face contorted and his powerful chest muscles twisting the fabric of his American polo shirt, shouted from one corner of the room into a microphone placed in the opposite corner, perhaps thirty feet away. From the control room, Konstantin waved signals to him like a symphony conductor. Then we listened to the cavernous, reverberating voice on the recording tape. The idea was that Gontzoff's booming voice would somehow overwhelm the jammers.

For a time, RL actually used the Konstantin-Gontzoff invention for some of its broadcasts. Daily programs for Soviet military garrisons across the border in East Germany would begin with Gontzoff shouting a stentorian salute, "Comrades, Soldiers, Officers, and Generals!" followed by a commentary on the topic of the day—the whole thing sounding like a general on a huge parade ground addressing his troops. Before long, however, we dropped the "technique" as of unproven effectiveness and, above all, absurdly hokey.

After leaving Munich, Vadim Gontzoff had a successful career as a classical-music disk jockey on a Long Island radio station, where he was able to speak normally.

Generally, we were so preoccupied with getting each day's programs ready by airtime that we had little time to think about jamming. Still, Soviet interference was a nuisance in more than one way. Not only did it interfere with reception of our programs by Soviet listeners, it also meant that we could not come home after a tiring shift at the station, settle back comfortably in an easy chair with a drink, and switch on the radio to review our day's handiwork. If we tried, all we ever heard was noise.

Still, jamming also had its positive effect on morale for us in Munich, one I'm sure the Soviets never intended. In moments of self-doubt, after a hard day of battling bureaucratic bosses and apathetic administrators, the jammers were always there, a constant reminder that in Moscow, at least, somebody really cared about our broadcasts.

What Can I
Tell You?

6

T he prime reason for Radio Liberty's existence was to tell listeners things about their own country that were suppressed by the government-controlled media.

How could we do this job? Arrayed against us was the awesome might of the Kremlin, intent on keeping uncensored information from getting out of the Soviet Union. What information about their country did we have to offer a doctor in Moscow, a schoolteacher in Noril'sk, a sheepherder in Kyrgyzstan, or a coal miner in Ukraine? As RL took to the air in 1953, that was our daunting challenge.

When I arrived in Munich in August 1952, someone had set up an "information section" staffed by a former operative of U.S. Army intelligence who had played games with the Soviets in Vienna, trying to pick up bits of information about their activities there while dodging the other side's sometimes brutal counter-measures. The idea of this section at RL was to extract information from "behind the Curtain" that could be carried in the broadcasts, as if we could use our shoestring resources to beat the KGB at its own game. At that time, we were also beset by individuals who, smelling profit from the American do-gooders at the new radio station, offered to supply us with news from networks of *Vertrauensleute* in Communist countries. Radio Free Europe, whose target countries were more open than ours, had been using these methods.

For us at RL, the pickings were slim. Occasionally, in those days before the Berlin Wall was built, a report would come out from East Germany about the activities of the Soviet garrisons there, but we seldom learned anything significant about the Soviet Union itself. In any case, these dredgings were hardly enough to sustain our broadcasts. Furthermore, there was always the question of reliability. Were the reports accurate, or was someone concocting them to make money from us? More ominously, was there a possibility of Soviet "provocations," false data leaked to us to make us look silly and damage our credibility?

Boris Shub was disdainful of this kind of news gathering. "Petty intelligence garbage," he called it, "produced either by fuck-ups or goniffs." Although some of the staff were eager to use such dubious but often sensational material, for the most part we kept them from doing so. Some of the items were patently phony, others questionable at best. As RL grew in professionalism, it formally adopted the journalistic "two source" rule: not to use news from offbeat sources unless there was independent confirmation from a second source deemed reliable.

Another potential information resource was defectors from the Soviet Union. These were few and far between. When they came they were useful in helping us keep in touch with the general situation in the Soviet Union, but they provided little hard news of consequence that we could use in programs. Some defectors broadcast moving appeals to their fellow citizens back home, affirming their love of their homeland and reciting the grievances against the system that had led them to leave, but these were one-shot contributions. One of the best was a statement by a Soviet Navy captain, Nikolai Fedorovich Artamonov, that I helped tape in Washington, D.C., around 1960. Artamonov, who lived in the United States under the name Shadrin, disappeared from view years later in Vienna, and it is now known that he died at the hands of the Soviets.

Over the years a considerable number of defectors joined the staff and became skilled broadcasters, helping to keep the station rejuvenated. One whose sustained contribution stands out is another naval officer, the modest and mild-mannered Lev Ivanovich Predtechevsky, whose informed commentaries on military topics were an RL staple for many years. But as news sources, defectors were of very limited value.

Because of RL's interest in defectors as potential radio talent, I used to run up by train to the U.S. government's Defector Reception Center near Frankfurt whenever a likely new person showed up. In Frankfurt I had an indirect brush with the long arm of Joe McCarthy. There I made friends with a State Department official, an affable Naval Academy graduate named Tom Ireland who had served in the Pacific during World War II and then in the Moscow embassy.

Ireland was deeply dedicated to his work, which involved reporting on the Soviet Union. He and his Russian-speaking wife Steena (daughter of a Dutch diplomat) threw wonderful parties for members of the Soviet affairs colony in the Frankfurt area, Americans and émigrés, with plenty of vodka and *zakuski* (herring, pickled mushrooms, beet-and-potato salad, a kind of eggplant spread called *baklazhannaya ikra,* and other toothsome hors d'oeuvres), at which someone usually played the guitar or balalaika while the guests sang Russian songs. The warmhearted Irelands always urged me to stay with them when I was in town and were helpful in many other ways. Then they disappeared from the scene, ostensibly because of a cut in the State Department budget. Back in Munich I tried to interest Manning Williams, then RL director, in hiring the talented but now unemployed Tom Ireland, but Manning demurred, mentioning that when they were both serving in Moscow Tom had borrowed his car and put a dent in it. He may have known (or sensed) what I learned only years later, that Tom's career had been ended after a State Department report noted that he and his wife "use Russian to a considerable extent in their household."

This horror story has a happy ending of sorts: Tom eventually established the real reason for his dismissal and in 1990 received a whopping settlement of $2.3 million from the government, but only after his marriage had broken up and he had fought (and finally won) a battle with alcoholism. He died in 1993 of lung cancer, having had little time to savor his victory.

In RL's earliest days, our sole news wire service was the Deutsche Presseagentur (DPA). Eventually we were also able to subscribe to the British Reuters service. Initially, the American news agencies would not sell us their service because we were a "propaganda outfit." The exception was the Hearst-owned International News Service (INS), but its output was in our eyes so inferior that we balked at paying the price. I remember a stormy encounter with the INS Bonn bureau chief, an American who came to my office and threatened to write negative stories about RL unless we subscribed. We held off in some trepidation, and the bureau chief never made good on his threat. Later, as RL's reputation improved through the addition to the staff of seasoned journalists such as Victor Ryser, United Press relented on having us as a client, and we received the INS service anyway when INS merged with UP as United Press International.

In those days the news agencies had relatively little to offer in the way of Soviet coverage. The few correspondents who were able to get accreditation in Moscow operated under advance censorship of their stories and severe restrictions on their activities. The *New York Times* used to warn its readers that stories from its Moscow correspondent, Harrison Salisbury, had been filed through censorship. DPA, in particular, was limited because Moscow had not yet recognized the Federal Republic as a state and so placed roadblocks in the way of West German correspondents.

All of this forced us to look creatively for new ways to cover the Soviet Union. For a long time, our mainstay was radio monitoring. The rectangular building at Oberwiesenfeld in which our studios were located had so many receiving antennas strung between the twin towers on its roof that they looked like the rigging of a ship. One of our monitoring resources was the TASS "Hellschreiber" system, which used captured German military equipment. We managed to get our hands on one of the Hellschreiber machines, a little box that received special radio transmissions in Russian from Moscow and turned them into purple marks in the form of letters on a narrow paper tape. The Hellschreiber transmissions were beamed to TASS clients in Eastern Europe and used an unfamiliar Russian transliteration based on Polish phonetics. Often TASS would move the news to Eastern Europe faster than to its own domestic clients, probably because the latter were entangled in additional layers of bureaucracy. By using Hellschreiber, we managed to score some journalistic coups on stories of interest to our listeners: we often got the news of government personnel shake-ups or decrees that radically affected their lives to our listeners before they heard it from Radio Moscow.

In the early hours of every morning, RL monitors (among them the bear trainer Il'yinsky, mentioned in the last chapter) would transcribe several hundred pages of voice broadcasts from Radio Moscow and other Soviet stations. This was an important resource because *Pravda* editorials, which each day set the latest party line, and all important decrees were read in full by announcers. By the time we arrived at the office at 9 A.M., we had a packet of such materials on our desks. That helped me become a speed-reader in Russian, since it was my job to summarize the monitoring output for our morning staff meeting. (Once, on my birthday, the monitors rewarded me with a special report: the Russian "Golden Alphabet," which they had transcribed from their collective memory. The "Golden Alphabet"– which, according to some authorities, was concocted about 200 years ago by Vasilii Pushkin, uncle of the famous poet–is a set of obscenely hilarious rhyming couplets, one for each letter of the alphabet. It was available from no printed source.)

Regional broadcasts from such cities as Kiev and Minsk were especially important, because they tended to be more outspoken about local problems, such as harvest failures or other sources of popular discontent, than were the blander central broadcasts from Moscow. By juxtaposing them in the form of "cross-reporting," we could come up with a more authoritative picture of what was happening in the country than listeners to Radio Moscow, or any other single radio station, were able to get.

Not long after RL went on the air, the monitoring section and the information section, together with the library and our fledgling research section, were merged into a new Information Department, which I headed (through various name changes) until 1960. I was particularly proud of the monitoring operation, a highly efficient operation that was the backbone of RL in the early years. Long after I left Munich, I was saddened to learn of allegations that the head of monitoring had been taking kickbacks from his employees in return for assigning them overtime. Although I knew nothing of this at the time, some of it must have happened on my watch, so I suppose I bear some of the responsibility.

Victor Frank, when he became head of RL's Russian desk, was a demanding user of the Information Department's output. He often complained to me that he needed more than we were giving him.

"Well, what would you do?" I asked him defensively one day.

Victor thought for a bit. "There's a chap in England who might be able to help you. He and I worked together during the war at BBC Monitoring."

The next thing I knew, Frank and I were at Munich's Riem Airport meeting a short, prematurely balding young man with a slight resemblance to early pictures of Vladimir Lenin. He had an air of shyness offset by a scarred upper lip that managed somehow to give him simultaneously a supercilious air. He was sweating in a heavy English suit much too warm for the weather that day.

"Jim Critchlow, this is Victor Zorza," Frank introduced us.

The retiring Zorza had little to say in the car riding back into Munich, but what there was came through in a peculiar blend of Polish-British accent.

Frank had already told me the essentials of Zorza's background. As a young man in the early days of the war, he had been evacuated from eastern Poland to the Soviet Union. He knew Russian well. When Stalin decided to allow the Polish general Władysław Anders to recruit Polish citizens for his army, Zorza had joined up and been taken to Britain, where he became an aviation cadet. He managed to crack up his training aircraft, receiving a severe blow to the head and being invalided out of the military. For the rest of the war, he worked as a monitor for the BBC.

Frank recalled to me how their fellow employees would laugh at Zorza during tea breaks when they would discuss their future after the war. "I go to write for Manchester *Guardian*," Zorza would say in broken English, to the general hilarity of the group, who scoffed at the idea that this uneducated Pole could ever appear in Britain's most prestigious newspaper.

Yet by the time Zorza came to Munich in 1953, he had established himself as a regular freelance contributor of Soviet affairs articles to the *Guardian*. From Munich Zorza continued his contributions. A secretary from the *Guardian* would telephone at prearranged times, and he would dictate his article. This often happened when he was having dinner at our apartment, a frequent occurrence before his redheaded English wife Rosemary came out from Britain to join him. I was awed by his recently acquired command of English, because as a rule the article would be unfinished when the call came, and I would hear him improvise the ending. Next day in the newspaper there it would be, exactly as he had dictated it. Zorza reminded me that "another" famous English writer, Joseph Conrad, was also a Pole.

For the next year and more, Victor Zorza was both the delight and the bane of my existence.

In my dealings with Zorza, two things quickly became apparent: first, his knowledge of Soviet reality, gained from years of on-the-scene suffering and insecurity, was light years ahead of my own, and second, he passionately believed that in a just world I would be the subordinate and he my superior, able to decide whether I was worth having around. I doubt, however, that he would have survived long in the American bureaucracy without me as a buffer. He had a way of getting into scrapes with people in the building, which I then had to smooth over. He strained the patience and good humor of my long-suffering secretary, Tatiana Hajek, whose charm, intelligence, and command of three languages were essential to the functioning of our office. (Frau Hajek, later Frau Venzl, survived both of us at RL, remaining in the office until her retirement many years later.)

Part of Zorza's resentment of me stemmed from the fact that it often fell to my lot to tell him that the American management was unwilling to accede to whatever request he had made of it. At times the requests were reasonable, at other times quite harebrained.

Victor was not one to conceal his feelings. "Come off it, Jim, don't be a mug," he would tell me impatiently whenever I made some remark that he considered particularly vapid.

Yet we continued to work together fairly harmoniously. For one thing, we both knew we had to get along. There was also a certain underlying liking between us, I feel sure. Each of us had encountered people in life for whom we had far less respect. Whenever I have seen Victor in the ensuing years, the greeting has been friendly, if tinged with a bit of the old strain.

I think that Zorza stayed in Munich as long as he did because he sensed, despite his resentment of me and other Americans whom he regarded as dilettantes, that we sincerely admired him and his work. After a few months his wife Rosemary joined him with their small son Richard (known then as Tinky) and their baby daughter Jane, and the family settled into a pleasant villa in the lakeside suburb of Gauting. By the time Victor finally returned to England, he had made a lasting contribution to the work of RL, one whose fruits are being harvested to this day.

The beginnings of Zorza's tenure were unpromising. I had already assembled a research section consisting of a small group of émigrés with varying degrees of literacy and skills. They were assigned to screen Soviet newspapers and report to me on what they found. Occasionally, I would learn something that I could pass on to the broadcasters.

Zorza made the research section his own, staying closeted with the staff all day behind closed doors. When I tried to find out what he was doing, he put me off impatiently. Finally, I questioned some of his people (who had reason to be grateful to me for hiring them) and was told that they were busy working on an "index." This was all very mysterious, but the staff seemed to have confidence in Zorza, so I decided to let matters take their course. But every day I chafed at the frustration of being left in the dark. Wasn't I the boss?

Weeks later, Zorza appeared triumphantly in my office waving a thick sheaf of paper: the index. It consisted of some 8,000 coded subject categories for gathering and classifying information on the Soviet Union. Zorza then proceeded to have his staff, who screened our intake of Soviet newspapers, about forty in all, also write abstracts of significant articles. The abstracts were duplicated in multiple copies, then color-coded, filed, and cross-filed according to the index categories. There were separate copies for each person mentioned (if he met criteria of importance), for each oblast (Soviet province), and for each subject category. A single abstract might require thirty or forty copies for cross-filing.

Over the years Zorza's archive yielded a massive, detailed data base on the Soviet Union. When a new party secretary appeared on the scene, we could trace his early career. If someone wanted information about wheat growing in Smolensk oblast, it was there for the asking. This laid the foundation of RL's research excellence. The number of categories has since had to be streamlined for practical reasons, but the system, renamed "Red Archive" by one of my successors, still bore Zorza's imprint many years later, even though most of those who worked with it were probably unaware of his role in creating it. (As a result of RL's new emphasis on research, our Information Department became the Soviet Research Department.)

After I left Munich the research department eventually came under Keith Bush, a spit-and-polish former British Army major who had commanded troops under fire in Malaysia. (Bush was a graduate of Sandhurst, to which I once referred in his presence as "Britain's West Point." "No," he corrected me, "West Point is America's Sandhurst.") Tiring of the military life and looking for a new challenge, Bush had gone to Harvard for courses in economics and Russian studies and had acquired U.S. citizenship. In Munich he diligently assembled a staff of first-class analysts with scholarly backgrounds to tap the Zorza archive. Under his leadership RL research rose to unprecedented heights of achievement.

In time Bush & Co.'s Munich research output was being read by leading Soviet affairs specialists in academe, government, and the media. In the late 1960s and early 1970s, when some forces in the United States sought to put RL and RFE out of business as "relics of the Cold War," RL received overwhelming support from Sovietologists who realized that this action threatened to destroy an invaluable Western source of information on the USSR. That support was crucial in keeping both stations alive. One State Department official even made the rather puzzling suggestion that RFE/RL programs be continued, only without putting them on the air, so that at least there would still be a reason for doing the research.

The prestige of RL's research continued to grow. Before it was eventually moved to Prague in 1994 as part of its post–Cold War incarnation, the facility's weekly report—which had been combined with RFE's research following the merger of the two stations—was commanding a subscription fee of $240 a year.

Long before all these happenings, Zorza had left us in the mid-1950s to return to England and new distinction as a journalist. He became a permanent staffer of the *Guardian* and a regular contributor to the *Washington Post.* With his ingenuity and intimate knowledge of Soviet life, he was able to score against his journalistic rivals. Once when the wire services were humming with news of a "popular" demonstration in Moscow against the American Embassy over some turn in U.S. foreign policy, Zorza picked up the telephone in his English office and called the local militia (police) station in Moscow. "What time is the demonstration due to end?" he asked in his fluent Russian. "At five o'clock," the militia officer at the other end told him, thinking that he was speaking to a Soviet official and not a British journalist. The *Guardian* headlined his story the next day, as evidence that in Moscow demonstrations were far from spontaneous.

Zorza's career took a sharply different turn after his daughter Jane died tragically of cancer as a teenager. Victor and Rosemary wrote a book about her ordeal and theirs, and became active in the hospice movement. Victor later went off to live in a village in India and stopped writing about the Soviet Union. The marriage broke up, and he gravitated to Leningrad, now St. Petersburg, where he became active in trying to create hospices for Russian terminal cancer patients. He is probably unaware that in 1993, just forty years after we first met, I was able to do him a good turn by giving positive information to a potential American financial contributor to his hospice movement, who happened to ask in my presence, "Who is this fellow Zorza? I've never heard of him."

In order to survive, the research department and the Zorza archive had to weather periodic budget cuts that targeted them for extinction. In the 1970s a senior executive, faced with a sharp reduction in RL's overall budget, took the position that it would be better for the station to eliminate research completely than to cut outlays for broadcasting; fortunately, Ronny Ronalds talked him out of it—not the least of his many contributions to RL's well-being.

As far as the Zorza archive was concerned, there was one major drawback in those early days of RL. While the world was beginning to discover and acclaim the research resource that he had created, in Munich the station's writers, for whom the archive had been conceived in the first place, tended to be lukewarm toward actually making use of it. Since most of them lacked previous journalistic training, it seemed easier to sit at a typewriter and write whatever came into their head than to go through the laborious process of assembling data from another source. The exception was BBC veteran Victor Frank, who became an avid consumer.

In general, there was a never-ending conflict of interest between broadcasters and researchers. The former, in the face of demands that they use the research product, wanted it to be written so that they could simply put it on the air with a minimum of adaptation. The researchers, on the other hand, countered that that would make them journalists, not researchers, and that you couldn't turn out reliable material if you had to worry about its impact on an audience. The dispute was still going on years later.

The trick of being a successful executive at RL was to take both sides in this dispute, and neither. Ronalds grasped this when he became program manager of RL soon after it went on the air in 1953 and in his later incarnation as the station's director. Many others did not, unfortunately, and this threw the station out of balance.

In the absence of research that could easily be cranked onto the air, the RL journalists were more apt to look elsewhere for their information. It seemed that if RL's scriptwriters were to use information from the research section, they would require spoon-feeding. We decided to try better packaging. Toward that end, I hired a slender, dark-haired young German who had come in looking for work. Dietrich Loeber had spent a year as a graduate student at Columbia University and spoke English. He had also learned Russian from his mother, a multilingual Latvian. Both languages were essential to our work.

With Loeber we created a publication called simply *Ezhenedel'nik* (Weekly). Most of Loeber's duties were menial: turning the crank of the ditto machine to run off stencils of various Russian-language materials or translations, stapling them together under a cardboard cover sheet, then distributing the copies from office to office.

Ezhenedel'nik served the purpose well, but after a time Loeber left to resume his studies. Today he is Professor Loeber of Kiel University, an authority on international law. When occasionally we meet at academic conferences, I remind him of his inauspicious beginnings, and we share a nostalgic laugh.

Those were days of exciting change in the Soviet Union, in the aftermath of Stalin's death and the ensuing jockeying for power among his successors. The situation created a tremendous thirst throughout the world for information about what was going on in the country. Boris Shub, who had returned to the New York office, kept peppering us with telexes clamoring for reports from the Munich "front line." It soon became evident that my shop had two jobs to do: to continue putting out information in Russian, RL's lingua franca, for use by the scriptwriters and also to produce high-quality English-language materials for the guidance of management, both in Munich and New York. In my ground-floor office I began to type out a daily analysis that went up to the brass on the second floor and from there was telexed to New York.

The response to my telexes far surpassed my expectation. I was told that on one occasion one of my reports had been placed the same day on President Eisenhower's desk. The telexes also began to appear as articles with my byline in publications like the *New York Herald-Tribune,* the *New Leader,* and the *Milwaukee Journal.* I wondered how they were finding their way into print.

Unknown to us in Munich, the New York office had hired a rotund, cigar-chomping journalist named Victor Lasky to do publicity for the radio. Casting about for material, Lasky latched onto my telexes and began to send them to editor friends. I finally met him when I came to New York on home leave in the summer of 1956, and thanked him for giving me a boost.

"I thought you must be somebody important," he said, looking me over, "but now I see you ain't." (I had just turned thirty.) Sure enough, my telexes kept popping up in print, but now without my byline.

Vic Lasky came from the same left-wing background as Boris Shub (he had once been editor of the *New Leader*) but had veered sharply to the right. He was no respecter of persons. He would sit in his tiny office hunched over a typewriter, a dead cigar clenched in his teeth. Although on the RL payroll, he also worked for other public relations clients, one of them the unsavory Dominican dictator Rafael Trujillo. His standard greeting when someone opened the door was to growl, "Fuck you!" without looking up from his typewriter to see who was there. Once Howland Sargeant, the Radio Liberty Committee's distinguished, white-haired, mild-mannered president, had happened into his office and received that treatment. Sargeant never came to see him again, but would send for him if he needed to talk to him.

After a brief stay at RL, Lasky left and wrote the best-selling *JFK: The Man and the Myth.* His hatred of the Kennedys was almost pathological. Once during the administration of President Richard Nixon, I ran into him on the street in Washington coming from the direction of the nearby White House. His face was split into a big grin.

"What's up, Vic?" I asked him.

"I've just seen some color photos of Jack Kennedy in bed with a girl, both naked," he chuckled. "Imagine!"

I despised Lasky's politics but could not help liking him personally, as did many of his journalistic colleagues to whom his views were anathema. In his personal dealings he was a straight shooter.

Dietrich Loeber's replacement as editor and general factotum of *Ezhenedel'nik* was another young Russian-speaking German. Christian Duevel had been a prisoner of war in the Soviet Union, where he worked as a *normirovshchik,* the man assigned to tally the prisoners' output to see whether they were fulfilling their production "norm." Following his release, he had spent a year in a clerical job in London. There he learned to write a pure English, although he spoke the language with a thick German accent. A bashful, soft-spoken, blond and baby-faced man, Duevel would blush scarlet at the least embarrassment.

Duevel's bashfulness was deceptive. From years of dealing with German Army superiors and then his Soviet captors, he knew subtle ways of besting higher authority. This ability figured in a singular incident that has stuck in my memory. It happened that I was summoned to the second-floor office of Robert F. Kelley, Otis Swift's successor as senior-ranking American at the station. Kelley was a former State Department official who in retirement had been sent to Munich to keep an eye on us. He was something of a historical monument, having been appointed in 1926 as the first head of the State Department's Division of Eastern Europe Affairs, where he assembled a splendid library of specialized reference works. It was Kelley who had collected the U.S. government's first cadre of Russian specialists by recruiting young men, such as Charles (Chip) Bohlen and George Kennan, then sending them off to Europe for intensive training in the language. (Both men later served as ambassadors to the Soviet Union.) Given the shenanigans of Swift and some of the other staff, Kelley's arrival in Munich brought fresh air to the scene. He was the upright, hard-working son of an Irish immigrant, and had managed to overcome disadvantages to graduate from Harvard in the class of 1915, with later study at the Sorbonne.

At the same time, Kelley had political scars. It seems that back in the 1930s some members of the Franklin D. Roosevelt administration got the idea that Kelley's State Department team of Russian experts was a detriment to good relations with the Soviet Union: they were always reminding the government of inconvenient facts about Stalin's regime. George Kennan tells in his memoirs how in 1937–ironically, the year of Stalin's Great Purge–Kelley's Division of Eastern Europe Affairs was eliminated, and how Chip Bohlen had to hide the most valuable works from its library in the attic of the department to evade orders to disperse them. During World War II, when good relations with the Soviet Union were crucial, Kelley was sent off to the U.S. Embassy in Ankara, supposedly out of harm's way. There he played bridge with fellow diplomats, including a Soviet named Vinogradov who was later (while I was assigned to Paris) Moscow's ambassador to France. The games often took place at the residence of the British ambassador. As the players chatted, drinks were served to the players by the valet, later unmasked as the German spy known as Cicero. Kelley used to describe the scene with a throaty chuckle. As for Communism, Kelley was bitter about people he considered wishy-washy on the Soviet Union, but at the same time he was a decent man who deplored Joe McCarthy's cutthroat tactics. He was at times critical of Roosevelt, but I discovered years later, when I would call on him in Washington after his retirement, that he had a signed photo of the late president displayed so that it was the first thing to catch a visitor's eye.

Although Kelley in Munich could be stern with wrongdoers, he was generally regarded as a benignly cheerful Irishman who kept out of people's way. His presence was seldom felt at my working level, so I was surprised to receive his summons one day.

When I reached Kelley's office, he was holding up the latest issue of our *Ezhenedel'nik*. "Look at this," he said.

"Yes, sir," I muttered.

"You've got a translation of an article in here by Harrison Salisbury of the *New York Times*."

It dawned on me that some people held it against Salisbury that he had filed copy through Soviet censorship while a Moscow correspondent of the *Times*. As Gay Talese wrote in his book about the *Times, The Power and the Glory*, Salisbury "was regularly attacked in the letters to the editor columns and in American magazines as being 'soft on Communism.'"

Kelley paused and looked at me. "Critchlow," he told me in his avuncular way, "don't ever let me see another article by Salisbury in your bulletin."

Unhappily but dutifully, I went back downstairs and told Duevel that "no more Salisbury" was the order of the day, thinking that would end the matter.

The next day Duevel shuffled into my office in his usual diffident way. "Mr. Critchlow," he asked, "may I see the index?"

"Index? What index?"

"The *Index Librorum Prohibitorum*," he told me, using the Vatican term for dramatic effect, "the index of forbidden works that has Mr. Salisbury's name on it." I studied his cherubic face for any hint of levity. There was none, but I had no doubt that somewhere inside he was laughing at our American pretensions of superiority.

With his quiet question, Duevel had managed to reduce Kelley (and me) to the level of heavy-handed censors. That was my first clue that I was dealing with an exceptionally subtle but forceful person.

One day Duevel handed me a well-written analysis of the latest shift in the Soviet party line. Not only was the analysis very solid, the English style was flawless.

"Who wrote this?" I asked him.

He turned lobster red. "I did," he said.

I was skeptical, given Duevel's heavily Germanic speaking style. "Let's see you do another one," I said. I put him in an adjoining room and waited. Within an hour, Christian came up with a new article, this one just as good as the first. I was convinced, and apologized for my doubts. Duevel began to write regularly for us.

That step launched an astonishing career. Duevel's analyses of the latest events in Moscow were eagerly awaited in chanceries throughout the Western world. Sometimes his views caused eyebrows to raise, but they were taken very seriously. Helmut Sonnenfeldt, who in the 1960s was head of "Soviet internal" in the State Department's Bureau of Intelligence and Research, told me once: "Duevel makes my hair stand on end at times, but I can't afford to miss a single line he writes." Later, when Henry Kissinger became secretary of state,

Sonnenfeldt rose meteorically to be counselor of the Department, one of its top career posts.

Unfortunately, Duevel's career was cut short by illness and early death, but not before he had made his mark in the annals of Western Sovietology.

No account of our Information Department in the 1950s can be complete without mention of John Greer Nicholson, a roly-poly Englishman who appeared in my office one day in quest of employment. A Cambridge graduate, Nicholson had an amazing command of Russian and other languages. He told me once that he would spend hours before a mirror perfecting his pronunciation, which required—he explained—exercising certain vocal muscles not used in English. Nicholson could chat easily with a Russian (or German or Frenchman) without having the latter suspect that he was not of the same nationality. He also had journalistic talent. I was happy to have him as a deputy, because he tried generously to make me look good even when he deserved the credit.

Although we became close friends, John always insisted on treating me formally in the office. The door connecting our two offices was kept open, but he would never enter my room without first knocking on the jamb. One day this made me impatient.

"Come on, John, you don't need to knock every time."

Nicholson looked heavenward and sighed. "Ah, Jim, the Englishman dies hard, you know."

To my great regret, John left Munich in a few years to sample life in North America. While working in the Russian Service of the Canadian Broadcasting Corporation in Montreal he obtained a Ph.D. in linguistics and, still a young man, was soon head of the Russian department at McGill University—another RL alumnus who went on to excel in other pursuits. He published a scholarly volume on Russian normative stress notation. Later, after serving for years as executive secretary of the Social Sciences and Humanities Research Council of Canada, he retired to the delightful community of Gananoque, Ontario, near the Thousand Islands, where he wrote regularly on Soviet and Russian affairs for Canadian newspapers until his death in 1995.

In trying to talk to Soviet listeners, there were agonizing dilemmas. How could we tell the truth about the Soviet Union without descending to the level of the other side's propaganda? When we read in *Pravda* that Soviet society was "the most democratic, the most humane in the world," that the Soviet citizen had a better life than his capitalist counterparts, it infuriated us. At the same time we realized that shouting back was not the way to deal with it.

One ingenious solution to this knotty problem came from Ted Weiant, a young American scholar and Russian linguist who appeared briefly on the Munich scene. To poke good-natured fun at the Soviet claim that the Communist Party's victories in single-party elections showed the superiority of the system, Weiant invented something he called "People's Democratic Football." Working with a Russian sports announcer and lots of sound effects, Weiant put on broadcasts of "people's democratic football matches." In this sport, there was only one team on the field. The listener would hear sounds of the crowd cheering and the announcer's ecstatic tally of the score as the team rolled up goal after goal, with no opponent.

The whimsical Weiant lived near me at one point, and we used to carpool. What I still remember in horror about the experience was his habit of browsing through magazines that he rested casually on the steering wheel while negotiating the perils of Munich traffic. He stayed only briefly in Munich before returning to the United States, where he later taught Russian and German at a small college in South Carolina.

RL's emerging excellence as an effective broadcaster to Soviet audiences was built by the lasting contributions of many people, both those like Weiant who appeared only fleetingly on the scene and hardy perennials, such as Alexander Schmemann and David Shub.

Alexander Schmemann was a Russian Orthodox priest who taught at the St. Vladimir Seminary in Tuckahoe, New York. Recruiting him was another of Boris Shub's great contributions to RL. Once a week for many years, Father Alexander came to RL's New York studios to tape a "Sunday talk." His breadth and sophistication enabled him to bridge the intellectual and spiritual gap between his church and his listeners who had been raised in the state ideology of atheism and taught in Marxist terms that all religion was "the opium of the masses." The priest avoided religious terminology, concentrating on moral and ethical questions that affect everyone, regardless of belief. His propensity for taking texts from Soviet Communist newspapers as his topic caused someone on the staff to label him jocularly as the "Komsomol priest," after the Soviet youth organization. Alexander Solzhenitsyn was one of Father Alexander's devoted listeners, calling him (as we later found out when Solzhenitsyn came to the West) "my favorite radio priest." (Schmemann's son Serge became a journalist, and by a fine historical irony reported the fall of Soviet power from the *New York Times* bureau in Moscow.)

Another contributor who put his stamp on RL was David Shub, Boris's father, who had come to the United States from Russia before the revolution. His early political leanings were toward the Menshevik faction, which broke with Lenin's Bolsheviks in 1903. He knew leading Russian politicians personally, an association that continued when many of them visited his New York apartment in the days before Lenin and Stalin clamped down on travel. As a writer on Russian politics for local Russian and Yiddish newspapers in New York, David maintained a lively interest in events in his native country. He was also known to English-language readers through his respected biography of Vladimir Lenin.

To David Shub, one of the spurious props of Soviet rule was the systematic distortion of Russian history that had become part of the official ideology. He and Boris reasoned that restoration of historical truth was an essential step to bringing Soviet society back to political health.

By the time RL went on the air in March 1953, David was ready with a series of programs on Russia's democratic heritage. His weekly series, one of the products of RL's New York program department, featured the democratic views of Russian writers from the past, such as Alexander Herzen and Vladimir Korolenko, whose works were either suppressed or distorted. To listeners indoctrinated by Marxist-Leninist propaganda to believe that Russia's tradition was entirely authoritarian, David's revelations about their history were as sensational as news of a major industrial accident in the Urals.

In another series of broadcasts aimed at party *apparatchiki,* David showed that Marxism as interpreted by Stalin was out of step with the views of many other figures in the mainstream of Marxist thought, from Georgii Plekhanov (the "founder of Russian Marxism") to Lenin himself to victims of Stalin's purges, such as Nikolai Bukharin. Without espousing any of these views, the RL series showed listeners the narrowness and intellectual sterility of Stalinist interpretations of Marx's ideology.

Although these broadcasts on "missing pages" of Russian history came from David's pen, the ideas were forged by interaction between father and son. David and Boris would meet on Sunday mornings at a designated street corner somewhere between their two homes in New York. There they would stand for hours, talking and gesticulating, sometimes raising their voices to make a point, David's restrained Old World manner in contrast to the brassiness of his New York–raised son.

Back in the office Boris, as head of RL's New York program center, was his father's boss. Such was the universal respect for David's work that this peculiar relationship never led to whispers of nepotism. David continued his weekly broadcasts over many years, coming regularly to the office until well into his eighties.

The people in this and earlier chapters were some of the many who gave RL an independent life and voice of its own. The money came from Washington, but the talent and dedication were their own precious resource.

Munich, "Center of Subversion"

7

I n Munich, there were actually three of us American broadcasters to the East, initially sheltered and supplied by the protective wing of the U.S. occupying power and able to draw for our personnel on the human reservoir offered by the accumulation in the area of displaced persons from the Soviet Union and Eastern Europe. With this concentration of resources, Munich became a routine target of Soviet propagandists, who invariably referred to the city as *diversionnyi tsentr* (center of subversion).

Housed downtown in the old U.S. Consulate-General on Ludwigstrasse, a concrete-stucco building confiscated from the Bavarian Agricultural Ministry, were the studios of the Voice of America's Munich Radio Center. In those early days, the consul-general who presided over the building was the flamboyant diplomat Charles Thayer, an old Russia hand who had written two books: *Bears in the Caviar* about his experiences in the 1930s when he helped set up the U.S. Embassy in Moscow and *Hands across the Caviar,* dealing with his later adventures in wartime Yugoslavia where he was parachuted as an American emissary to Tito's partisans. Like their author, the books were entertaining but with an underlying seriousness. Charlie Thayer was a bluff, likable eccentric who received visitors in his stocking feet and at the end of the day would slide down the building's curving banister from his fourth-floor office, to the awe and astonishment of German visa applicants gathered in the atrium below. He addressed all males who were not close acquaintances as "pal." One day when I happened to encounter him, he asked me out of the blue: "Say, pal, what do you think of the political role of the Soviet military?"

Knowing from *Bears in the Caviar* that Thayer was a West Point graduate who had hobnobbed in Moscow with such important Soviet military figures as Marshal Semyon Budyonny, I believe I had the good sense to sidestep his question.

Sadly, Thayer fell victim to the demagogical senator Joe McCarthy, all because his sister Avis happened to be married to another U.S. diplomat, Charles Eustis Bohlen, who had been President Roosevelt's interpreter at Yalta in 1945. When President Eisenhower infuriated McCarthy in 1953 by nominating Bohlen as ambassador to the Soviet Union without first consulting the senator, McCarthy decided to torpedo Bohlen's confirmation by the Senate. Since he could find nothing in Bohlen's distinguished record to use against him, he let it be known that he would "get" him through his brother-in-law Charlie Thayer, who had committed the indiscretion—such things loomed terribly large in those hysterical days—of having had Russian girlfriends during his service in Moscow. Rather than be used as a weapon against Bohlen, Thayer suddenly tendered his resignation. He retired to a mountain retreat near Ruhpolding, Bavaria, and succeeded in writing some more good books and articles before his death. Chip Bohlen and Avis moved into Spaso House, the U.S. ambassador's residence in Moscow, where he served with distinction; from Moscow Avis would write her brother back in Bavaria letters containing tidbits from the local scene.

As consul-general, Thayer had had little to do directly with VOA's operations, although in 1947 he had played a seminal role in setting up its first Russian broadcasts. VOA's Munich Radio Center originated programs in Russian and other Communist-bloc languages to supplement those coming from the main studios in Washington, and its activities were controlled from there. It was easy for us to keep up with what VOA was doing in its Russian broadcasts because its medium-wave and low-wave transmitters located in Bavaria were well audible in Munich. In those days VOA, especially its Munich branch, was a militant weapon in the Cold War, not at all like the sedate instrument of U.S. "public diplomacy" that it became later on. Often, one might tune in one of its newscasts and hear a stentorian voice leading off with an item like this: "Listen carefully! We now broadcast the latest revolutionary order of the NTS!"

The "revolutionary" NTS was headquartered in Frankfurt-am-Main, four hours up the Autobahn from Munich. One of the differences between VOA and RL in those early days was that after we went on the air we gave the NTS a wide berth so as not to compromise the objectivity of our programs. This exposed us to criticism from some quarters as being only halfheartedly anti-Communist. Evidently the leadership of VOA, which was subject to direct congressional scrutiny, thought it prudent to pull out all the anti-Communist stops in that troubled era of McCarthyism, even to becoming a mouthpiece of the NTS. At RL we too worked in constant fear of being singled out by McCarthy as one of his targets, but it never happened. In the poisonous atmosphere of those days, there was a paradox that few outsiders appreciated: the shield provided by RL's intelligence ties helped it to remain a calm, reasoned voice, to avoid becoming a frenzied, hard-hitting propaganda outlet. McCarthy took on VOA's parent, the U.S. Information Agency, as well as the State Department and the army, but he steered clear of the CIA. Still, it was the conventional wisdom for decades, even among government people who should have known better, that *we* were the heavies of the Cold War.

The head of the VOA's Munich Russian service was another Charlie, a colorful Californian named Charles Malamuth who had enlisted in the Canadian Army in 1917 so that he could go to Siberia with its expeditionary force in the hope of finding a lost relative. He never found the relative but returned safely to California with a store of memories. Later, in the 1920s and 1930s, he worked in Moscow as a journalist. One of his stories of that period was about acquiring a handsome Russian *shuba* (a fur winter coat); seeing the coat, ordinary Russians would assume that he was a *barin,* an aristocratic holdover from the old regime, and come up to him to ask for help against the Communists. He was embarrassed (and saddened) by one old peasant babushka who clutched his coat in desperation and shouted, "Barin! Barin! Help us, they're trying to drive us into the collective farm!"

Affable Charlie Malamuth, a stout, balding bon vivant, was a master of bureaucratic infighting. In 1953 Senator McCarthy's two young henchmen, Roy Cohn and David Schine, made their infamous tour of U.S. government installations in Western Europe. In the atmosphere of terror that then reigned thanks to their boss, officials along their way had good reason to fear becoming arbitrary victims and losing their careers. When the two travelers arrived in Munich, most Americans went to great lengths to stay out of their way. In contrast, the wily Malamuth fastened them in his paternal grip and took them to a VIP guest house for a secluded weekend. Shortly after Cohn and Schine returned to Washington, it was announced that VOA would suffer budget cuts except for its Munich operation, which would have its funding increased.

I called on Malamuth in his office early one morning soon after my arrival in Munich to see what I could learn about running a Russian radio station. He greeted me warmly and was helpful and attentive for the whole day.

Even in those Cold War days, most of us at RL thought VOA's blatant propaganda approach was off the mark. Still, my day with Malamuth taught me a lot about the mechanics of getting a broadcast on the air. (Later on, after he joined RL himself as the result of a personnel cut at VOA, we became close friends and frequent luncheon companions, although often disagreeing on work issues.) Despite our political differences, we at RL always seemed to enjoy good relations with our opposite numbers at the Munich VOA, helped along by common audience interests and personal alliances, such as the marriage between Zhuk Obolensky of our newsroom and Lyudmilla (Lucy) Chernova, VOA's gorgeous Russian announcer whose richly sensuous voice might give even a Politburo member thoughts of defection to the West.

For various reasons, our relations with the third of the American radio stations in Munich were never that cordial. Radio Free Europe had been broadcasting successfully to the "captive nations" of Eastern Europe ever since 1950. Its audiences, enslaved by Communist regimes imposed on them after World War II by the bayonets of the Red Army, were eager for any message of hope from the West. To do its job, RFE had assembled a competent coterie of professional journalists, exiles from the five countries (Poland, Czechoslovakia, Hungary, Romania, and Bulgaria) to which it beamed its programs. This staff spoke English, often with a British inflection that sounded lofty in our American ears. Its linguistic sophistication enabled RFE's American executives to conduct meetings in their own language.

The experienced journalists of RFE's newsroom distributed, in English, a comprehensive and informative daily news "budget" of several hundred pages to the exile staffs. RFE research, also distributed in English, was equally impressive.

When RL began to appear on the Munich scene in 1952, the general reaction at RFE seemed to be one of contempt. To most of the neatly dressed Poles, Czechs, and others who worked in RFE's sleek quarters on the edge of Munich's English Garden, our Soviet audiences were the enemy, their oppressors, and broadcasting to them was a waste of time and money that could be better spent to beef up RFE. They were equally disdainful of the threadbare gaggle of inexperienced DPs that we had assembled from the camps around Munich. I can still see the way one executive at RFE curled his lip when I told him that at RL we Americans had to run our meetings in Russian, the only language that a majority of the staff could comprehend. (We thought that was not a bad thing, since it kept the management of the operation closer to the audience.) To many Eastern Europeans who had witnessed the coarse and often cruel behavior of the Red Army in their homelands, RL's heavy concentration on intellectual and cultural programming—the result of Boris Shub's influence—was a patent absurdity. Who would listen to it? The idea of "Russian culture" was to them an oxymoron; even those who respected past Russian greats like Tolstoy or Dostoyevsky argued that their attainments had nothing to do with the contemporary Russians they knew, who were robbers and rapists. There were worthy exceptions, however, such as Jerzy Giedroyc, editor of an intellectual Polish-language journal in Paris, who regularly devoted space to Russian cultural developments, and the Pole Leo Labedz who edited the English-language review *Survey* in London.

Those Eastern European feelings of superiority toward our Soviet nationalities rubbed off on RFE's American executives, compounded by the latter's realization that RL funding and theirs came out of the same government pocket. This put us in direct competition for resources and made RL appear a threat in the eyes of some of them. Not long after RL went on the air, I happened to meet a journalist named Franz Spelman who worked for RFE; he confided that our new station had become known familiarly throughout his organization as Radio Hole-in-the-Head.

Another source of this smugness toward RL was the fact that RFE was far better known to the American public. Its mass fund-raising campaigns using radio, television, and billboards had made it a household word in the United States. Even schoolchildren were urged to contribute their pennies to help the broadcasts. When much later it came to light that most of RFE's funding had come covertly from the government, there was a reaction of outraged surprise from people who had believed RFE's claims that it was privately supported. In the Senate Foreign Relations Committee, Frank Church of Idaho, who had once been gulled into escorting citizens of his state to Munich on a fund-raising junket, steadfastly voted against legislative efforts to keep RFE (and RL) alive after their CIA funding was terminated. Fortunately, RL never asked American schoolchildren for their pennies or engaged in other forms of mass solicitation, although it, too, was not candid about its sources of financing. The lower profile had its price: even after RL had been broadcasting for some years, few Americans could tell you what it was.

It was only after Soviet troops shed much blood in 1956 to put down the Hungarian uprising that some Eastern Europeans began to accept the idea that liberation of their countries would not be possible without preliminary political change in Moscow. Shortly after the massacre, I attended a Munich speech by an émigré Hungarian writer who made the sardonic point that if ever there was a Budapest-style anti-Communist uprising in Moscow, it would not be put down by troops from Hungary. His point was eventually proved, but not until the successful popular overthrow of the Soviet regime in 1991.

Eventual recognition that Eastern Europe's liberation was dependent on change within the Soviet Union brought marginally greater acceptance, even by Poles and Czechs, of the importance of broadcasts to the Soviet Union. This led to a curious anomaly: without actually saying so, some RFE spokespersons began to imply that their station broadcast to the entire Soviet bloc. I was present at one public forum where an RFE representative twisted and turned to sidestep the admission that his station did not carry programs in Russian. In hindsight, such shenanigans seem merely trivial and silly, but at the time they stung us.

When the RFE people stuck to their own mission, they did extremely well. The enthusiastic reception given many of their microphone personalities when, after the collapse of Communism, they were finally able to visit their audiences has left little doubt of that. But when RFE executives tried to meddle in the affairs of Radio Liberty and the complex business of broadcasting to Soviet audiences, they were often out of their depth. The difference in approach between the two organizations was brought home after 1971, when the CIA got out of the picture and the White House and Congress decided to consolidate them under one corporate roof. The ensuing struggle over division of resources and turf led to an outpouring of acrimony. When a veteran RFE executive was placed in charge of RL programming, the results were disastrous. But I am getting ahead of my story.

The Hungarian uprising caused a shake-up at RFE after it came to light that Hungarian listeners to its broadcasts believed that U.S. military forces would help them in their rebellion against Soviet hegemony. Although later investigations uncovered "policy violations" by individuals, there was no evidence of a systematic management effort to foment rebellion. But the heat was on. One apparent consequence was that RFE's American policy advisor, William Griffith, returned shortly thereafter to the United States, where he taught at MIT and Tufts University, and became a roving editor of *Reader's Digest*.

There were some valid reasons that made it harder for RL to do an effective job than for RFE. Despite the Iron Curtain lowered by the Soviets, Eastern Europe was relatively more open to the West than was the heartland of Communism, the USSR. There were also subjective factors that made RFE's job easier. In addressing audiences that identified with the West and saw themselves as victims of foreign occupation by the Russians, RFE was knocking at an open door. In contrast, the main thing our RL audiences knew about the West was that the Nazi invasion had come from that quarter in 1941. Moreover, Soviet citizens ever since 1917 had been in the grip of a propaganda and terror machine that tried to achieve total thought control over them. It drummed into them that their system was the most humane and the most generous in the world, threatened only by the "capitalist encirclement" represented, inter alia, by Radio Liberty.

At RL we had a special problem: the tendency of many in the audience to view our émigré staffs as traitors to their homelands. Soviet propaganda played on this feeling by portraying our people as "war criminals." In nearly every case, such accusations were fabricated. In a few instances, some germ of fact lay beneath the tissue of distortion, though most often with extenuating circumstances—coercion by the Nazis, for example—about which the Soviet propagandists were silent. Over the years only a small handful of cases came to light where we had reason to believe that an RL colleague had willingly committed criminal acts under the Nazis—discoveries usually made after the individuals in question had died or left our employ. Strangely enough, Soviet propagandists were less apt to play up these truly troublesome and embarrassing cases, preferring to level their charges at the innocent—a clear indication that they were less interested in getting at the truth than in discrediting and demoralizing RL.

For Americans of my generation, many of us World War II veterans, there was initially something distasteful about having to associate with people who had worn German uniforms, whether or not they had committed war crimes. Yet there were scores of such people in our building at Oberwiesenfeld.

Wolfgang Koehler helped put this problem in perspective for me.

That was the false name used to protect his family back in Moscow by Georgii Yakovlevich Protazanov, a former Red Army soldier who worked at RL in Munich as a producer. His father, Yakov Aleksandrovich Protazanov, was one of the best-known Soviet film producers. Born in 1881, the elder Protazanov was a successful filmmaker before the revolution, with seventy-five titles to his credit. After 1917 he managed to continue his career through the twists and turns of Stalin's cultural policies. He even managed to live down the fact that he and his family had spent some time in France—the kind of exposure that in other cases had led Stalin to have people shot for "treason" and "espionage." I once saw a revival of one of Protazanov's films, *The Feast of St. Jurgen,* made in 1930; it was notable among Soviet cinematographic output for its lightheartedness and the excellence of its photography.

Young Protazanov's use of a false identity at RL to protect his family seems to have succeeded. An official anthology of his father's articles on the cinema was brought out in 1957, and in 1959 the ten-volume Soviet "Small" Encyclopedia *(Malaya Entsiklopediia)* carried a biographical entry for him (featuring a photo portrait that bore a striking likeness to his son Georgii). Both of these circumstances were a sure sign of official favor, although during that time Georgii's career at RL was in full bloom. Georgii's father had died in August 1945, but the fate of his mother and others continued to concern Georgii.

We all knew the young Protazanov as Groggi, a nickname that had stuck to him after the war. Later I learned that the name Groggi was the result of his German wife Tilly's attempts to pronounce his real Russian name, Georgii. When the two of them joined us in Munich in the fall of 1952, I knew little of Groggi's background except that his recruitment had been pushed by Boris Shub, who spoke highly of his character and talent. Groggi, a lean, dapper, fresh-faced man with athletic good looks, quickly won us over with his fun-loving charm. Only when I came to know him better did I discover that beneath his cheerful exterior there was an underlying sadness, the pang of having a false identity, of being separated from home and loved ones, coupled with the awful realization that any effort to bridge the gap and reestablish communication could lead to dire consequences for those concerned.

My friendship with Groggi ripened after Stalin's death, when he was one of those assigned to go with me for a few days to the transmitter base in distant Lampertheim, an adventure I have described earlier. We worked together on other occasions after that. I remember in particular one grueling all-night drive through fog to return to Munich from Bern, where we had been covering the European Track and Field Championships.

To my dismay, I heard one day that Groggi had helped make films for the Germans during the war. I wondered how an anti-Fascist like Boris Shub could have recommended a person like that to RL in such cordial terms. Once when Groggi and I were relaxing together, I asked him about it point-blank.

"Groggi," I blurted out, "is it true that you made films for the Nazis?" hoping that he would deny it.

"Yes," he sighed. "I'm afraid it's true."

"But how could you?" I asked.

"All right, I'll tell you," he answered, "but you'll have to promise not to interrupt until I've finished my story."

I learned that Groggi, an apprentice in the Soviet film industry, had patriotically joined the Red Army after the German invasion in June 1941, without waiting for conscription. He was sent to the front line almost immediately, at a time when the German advance was rapid. As his unit retreated in haste, he was wounded in the leg and left by his comrades in a ditch beside the road.

"Help me," he begged his fleeing fellow Russians. "Don't leave me to the Germans."

Groggi's pleas were ignored. He lay in the ditch, fearing instant death or torture from the German troops when they arrived. To his amazement, the first German soldiers he saw called an ambulance and had him taken to a military hospital behind their lines. A German surgeon operated on his leg, and he was placed in a clean hospital bed.

Groggi's recovery from surgery took six months. During that time he was free to hobble around the surrounding area on a stick. He explained to me that this was a period, just after the outbreak of the war, when the military were in full control of occupied territory, before Nazi politicos took over and the SS was given free rein. The German military commander in this sector happened, according to Groggi, to be a decent and enlightened man. He dissolved the Soviet collective farms and left the peasants pretty much to their own devices. The result was a rebirth of agriculture depressed by Stalin's "reforms" and a new prosperity in the area.

This improvement in conditions so impressed Groggi, he told me, that when at the end of his convalescence the Germans, who had learned of his background, offered to send him to Berlin to make propaganda films, he accepted without hesitation. It was only after arriving in Berlin that his eyes were opened and he began to see the true face of the Third Reich. Some of the German filmmakers with whom he was assigned to work turned out to be secret enemies of Hitler. Before Groggi knew it, he was involved in an anti-Nazi underground. One of those he met was Tilly, a Berlin girl who was half Jewish. Through his connections, Groggi was able to help her escape persecution. They fell in love and were married.

At the war's end, conditions in Berlin were very bad. Tilly fell ill, and there was no food or medicine. In desperation Groggi went to the American Military Government. He stumbled into the office of Melvin Lasky, a young New York intellectual who was a friend of Boris Shub, and made a plea for help. Learning of his background as a Russian prisoner of war, Lasky asked one question: "What did you do after you were captured?"

"I made movies," Groggi replied.

"What, movies? For the Nazis? Then get the hell out of here, or I'll have the MPs throw you out." That was Lasky's reply as related to me by Groggi.

Somehow Groggi managed to persuade Lasky to give him five minutes to tell his story. When he came to the part about the anti-Nazi underground and his ailing half-Jewish wife, Lasky relented. He picked up the telephone and called his wife Brigitte. "Bring the car," Groggi heard Lasky tell her. "There's someone here whose wife needs help. I want you to take him to the PX."

In short order, the two couples were close friends. Through the Laskys, Groggi and Tilly met their other friends Boris and Libby Shub. (Boris's younger brother Anatole later married Lasky's younger sister Joyce.)

Not every former Soviet's wartime history was as easily explained as Wolfgang Koehler's. Some units of Soviet prisoners of war organized by the Germans were assigned to police duties in occupied territories, and there is little doubt that some of them committed

Boris Shub as RL policy advisor, around 1955. Shub urged us to be "democrats with a small 'd'" and to despise all propaganda, Communist or anti-Communist. (Courtesy Anatole Shub.)

Above: Heads of the RL language desks, around 1960: Torossian (Armenian), Rossinsky (Russian), Dobriansky (Ukrainian), Zunnun (Turkestani), Akber (Azerbaijani), Khodarov (North Caucasian), Cvirka (Belorussian), Josefoglu (Tatar-Bashkir). (Courtesy RFE/RL Inc./Tanja Venzl.) **Left:** Aza, a North Caucasian who worked in RL's tape library. From time to time, the public relations office would ask her to put on native costume and pose as a "broadcaster." She also assisted audience research by luring Soviet citizens to interviews. She married Wytold Ryser of the news desk, later Paris bureau chief. (Courtesy RFE/RL inc./Tanja Venzl.) **Right:** A staff party in the early days. The piggyback rider is Pulitzer prizewinner Edmund Stevens. (From author's personal archive.)

Russian Broadcaster Leonid Pylayev entertaining executives, undoubtedly as the butts of his humor. Ronny Ronalds is fifth from left. (Courtesy Francis Ronalds.)

RL was housed during its first years in the former operations building of the old Munich airport. In 1938, British and French representatives landed here to negotiate the giveaway of Czechoslovakia. (Courtesy RFE/RL Inc./Tanja Venzl.)

Left: The author, circa 1955, trying to concentrate in the corner office which was a target of buzzing German pilots. (From author's archive).

Upper left: Audience research wizard Max Ralis (From author's archive.)
Upper right: Russians poked fun at the author for trying hard to master their culture. (From author's archive.) The drawing is by Nikolai Menchukov, shown **(below)** with a group of Russian staffers in the RL library. Menchukov, a freelance writer for the Russian desk, was famous among the staff for his irreverent caricatures. (Courtesy RFE/RL Inc./ Tanja Venzl.)
Right: Pylayev and Yul Brynner in *The Journey*. (Courtesy RFE/RL Inc.)

Upper left: Russian-born former Polish diplomat Wytold Ryser, ex-Soviet army officer Lev Korneichuk, and Paris taxi-driver turned novelist Gaito Gazdanov, all RL news staffers. (Courtesy RFE/RL Inc., Tanja Venzl.) **Above:** Victor Frank, for years on-air broadcaster and influential behind-the-scenes policymaker, always a voice for moderation. (Courtesy Vasily Frank.) **Left:** Ronalds and Alexander Bacherach debate a point at 1962 sendoff to Paris for the author (between them in background). (From author's archive.) **Below:** Ronalds and the author celebrating the end of the Cold War in Moscow, 1991. (Courtesy Jon Sawyer.)

atrocities against civilians. Ironically, most of the units of ex-Soviets were never used in action, because Hitler looked down on and distrusted them.

Stalin never forgave Soviet citizens who fell into German captivity, whether or not they agreed to serve their captors. He spurned efforts through the Red Cross to better their conditions. He even refused the opportunity to get help for his own son, Yasha, who was taken prisoner by the Germans and later died in a camp. When after the war former prisoners were repatriated by the Allies to the Soviet Union, Stalin's regime treated them as criminals, regardless of their wartime conduct.

Talking to former prisoners gave me a better understanding of what had led so many of them to agree to work for the Germans. Partly because of Stalin's unwillingness to cooperate with the Red Cross, they watched their comrades die in droves from malnutrition and disease. Yet their treatment by the Germans was not radically worse than what they had undergone in the Soviet Union during collectivization or in the gulag; even if they had not experienced the gulag personally, they knew of it through relatives and friends. To such people, putting on the uniform of one of the special units organized by the Germans did not seem such an immoral act, especially if it was the only way to escape death from starvation.

Former Soviet citizens had only a hazy notion of Nazi atrocities. To be sure, they had heard of them from their own propaganda, but the Soviet media were so mendacious in other respects that citizens tended to discount what they were told, even when it happened to be true. A Central Asian Muslim told me he had been surprised to learn that a large number of his fellow Muslims had been shot on orders of a German commander when it was discovered that, like all good Muslims, they were circumcised; the German commander assumed from this fact that they must be Jews and had them killed. "Until then," my Muslim friend told me, "we didn't know that the Nazis were anti-Semitic."

That is not to say that there were no war criminals among those who fell into German hands during the war. But, as the case of Georgii Protazanov demonstrated, it was certainly not true that every former "collaborator" was a war criminal.

Who's Listening?   8

E ver since RL first took to the airwaves in March 1953, we had wondered whether anyone in the Soviet Union actually listened. For us in Munich, turning on the radio to RL's frequencies was unsettling, because the only sound we ever heard was the ugly rasping of the Soviet jammers. We had no way of knowing that our broadcasts, weak as they were, already had an audience, even in the gulag. It took us twenty-one years to find out from a former political prisoner named Alexander Solzhenitsyn that he had been a regular listener "from the start of RL." That is what he told Ronny Ronalds, by then RL's director, when he came to the West in 1974. Nor did we dream that the day would come when "Radio Hole-in-the-Head" would number among its listeners a general secretary of the Communist Party of the Soviet Union, Mikhail Gorbachev, struggling in 1991 as a prisoner in his Crimean dacha to learn what was happening to the Moscow putsch.

Frustrating as they were, RL's early efforts to learn about its audience entered a new stage in 1956. We received word by telex from the New York office that someone named Max Ralis was headed for the Munich scene, evidently with high-level sponsorship. Ralis, the telex told us, had left New York by boat. This mysterious character would be in charge of audience research for RL. No further details.

This news wounded me. Up to then, audience research—such as it was—had been one of the responsibilities of my Information Department. Ralis's appointment was a clear vote of no confidence in our efforts. At the same time, my feeling of hurt pride was tinged with relief: I had plenty of other work and was glad to see someone else saddled with the daunting challenge of finding out how many people in the vast expanse of the Soviet Union could be counted as RL listeners.

It was probably just as well that in those days we had no idea of how large or small the audience was. Knowing the real size of the audience for our feeble transmitters would doubtless have discouraged us even more. Only in 1960, with the addition of more powerful transmitters in Spain, did we improve our competitive position against the jamming network.

Still, we were desperate from the first to get any evidence of listening that we could. For some reason, the responsibility was given to me, probably because the task looked hopeless and no one else wanted it. Joan de Wend Hunt, a willowy, witty Cambridge graduate who had joined us in Munich after a brief career in the British foreign service, was assigned to help me. Together, we tortured our gray cells.

In those days before the Berlin Wall was built, the border between the Soviet Zone of Germany and the Western sector of Berlin was not so tightly sealed. As I mentioned earlier, we rented mailboxes in West Berlin, then broadcast the addresses with an invitation to listeners to write. Periodically, a German employee would go around to check for letters. We hoped that at least one member of the Soviet occupying force in East Germany might find an opportunity to drop something into the mail that would slip past the Communist postal censors. Anxiously, we waited and waited. "Keep your pecker up," Joan encouraged me one day as I left her office, stopping me dead until I remembered that that gem of British slang has nothing to do with the male anatomy.

Occasionally a letter would turn up in one of the boxes, but it would be from some homesick refugee in the West who had heard our Russian program and was writing in the hope of establishing contact with fellow countrymen. Once we even had a letter from a Russian in Communist China, but nothing from the Soviet Union.

It was well over a year before we heard from our first bona fide Soviet listeners, the two men mentioned in an earlier chapter who scrawled only their first names on a postcard bearing the postmark of Brest on the Soviet-Polish border. As I said, we thought they might be soldiers on their way home from the Soviet Zone of Germany; we knew from a monitoring station set up in Berlin, in the middle of the zone, that our broadcasts could be heard there, if with difficulty. The postcard must have caught the censors napping, but they soon woke up again, and it was many months before another piece of authentic Soviet mail came in.

We were also hoping to receive recognition for our broadcasts in the form of attacks in the Soviet press. With rare exceptions in those early days, however, the Soviets were too cagey to give us free publicity in their own media.

If this state of affairs was frustrating for us in Munich, it was even more so for Howland Sargeant, president of the Radio Liberty Committee back in New York. Sargeant was being peppered with questions in Washington about whether the dollars going into RL were producing any listeners. Finally, as I later learned, he had decided to take matters into his own hands and, with an assist from Boris Shub, found and hired Max Ralis.

Joan Hunt was even more stirred than I by the news of Ralis's impending arrival. Her assignment with me had liberated her from the drudgery of RL's translation section. She seemed to find my office congenial and was shocked when I told her that in future she would be reporting to the unknown Ralis, not to me. She even accused me of tossing her over the side and glared in disbelief when I tried to explain that the situation was beyond my control.

The days passed with agonizing slowness as Ralis's ship seemed to inch across the Atlantic. When finally he reached Munich, he increased our suspense still further by staying away from the office for several days on personal business. From members of the administrative staff who were helping Ralis to settle in, a few scraps of information began to filter back to us: he was forty-one, divorced, a U.S. citizen, and spoke many languages. Gradually, we pieced together more: he was Moscow-born, had gone to school in Berlin, had been a rug salesman in Paris and a taxi driver in New York, and had served in two armies, French and American. With his sister and a girlfriend, also Jewish, he had walked across the Pyrenees into neutral Spain under the noses of France's Nazi invaders. He had also studied sociology in Germany and, just before coming to Munich, had spent a year doing fieldwork in a village in India. Fieldwork in an Indian village? What did that have to do with RL? Only later, after Max had settled in, did we learn that when the war ended he had attended courses at Columbia taught by another immigrant, the well-known sociologist Paul Felix Lazarsfeld, who in the pretelevision age had made a name for himself, among other things, for his studies of the impact of radio broadcasting on mass audiences.

At last the suspense ended for me when Ralis finally showed up in my office. The ogre I had imagined turned out to be a short, smiling man who radiated warmth and humanity. He held out a piece of paper, and I recognized Boris Shub's unmistakable scrawl.

"The bearer of this is a solid citizen," I read. "See what you can do to help him." Ralis's late father, it turned out, had been, like Shub's father David, a Menshevik. One of Max's earliest childhood memories was of being taken, when about six years old, to visit his father in a Moscow jail.

That evening Ralis had dinner at my home—an event that marked the beginning of many years of friendship. As for Joan Hunt, she was so charmed by his French manners and his resemblance to Claude Rains, the British actor best known for playing the French police chief in *Casablanca,* that she instantly forgot her pique at having to leave me.

Max quickly became an accepted part of our little social world. Still, when he began talking about his plans to study the audience, we began to doubt his grip on reality. How did he intend to go about it? we asked. Why, by using standard social science techniques, he told us. What you had to do was interview a representative sample of listeners, and from that you could project the audience size and other parameters.

"Max," we told him. "That's crazy. You can't interview people in the Soviet Union."

"I know," he explained patiently. "You have to catch them when they're traveling abroad."

That did little to reassure us about Max's sanity. We knew that RFE had been using this technique, but travelers from the Eastern European countries were much less supervised, and much less skittish about talking to foreigners, than were our Soviet audience. In those days, with the spy mania of the Cold War raging, the few Soviet citizens who were allowed abroad traveled in carefully watched packs. In each group were always some who had covert ties to the security police and orders to report any indiscretions, especially unauthorized conversations with foreigners. Not only that, but each member of the group was held reponsible for the conduct of all others. If someone failed to report that a comrade had gotten out of line, that person would be regarded as an accomplice.

Another thing made us skeptical about Max's scheme. Most Soviet travelers abroad were officials sent by the party and government, presumably people of outstanding loyalty to the regime. Later on, ordinary Soviet tourists began to visit foreign countries, but they too underwent rigorous loyalty checks, were kept tightly supervised, and invariably had to leave a spouse or other family member behind as hostage.

The worst part of Max's ideas was that he presented them in a weird language that tended to undermine the confidence of his American associates. Not only was his English peculiar, but also he came close to having no mother tongue at all. The only language he spoke without accent was German, thanks to elementary schooling in Berlin, but before he could achieve a mature command of it the Nazis had caused the family to flee to France.

Max's guttural pronunciation of French had caused him serious problems while serving in the French Army early in World War II. His unit was assigned to the Maginot front facing the German Army, and Max was made a bicycle courier, carrying dispatches back and forth. Once some French military policemen stopped him to check his identity. A few words of his French were enough to convince them that they had caught a German spy, and they locked him up. Before he could be shot, his commanding officer came to identify him, and he was released.

Max sounded quite intelligent in French or Russian, despite having the same atrociously guttural accent in both languages. I never understood why his pronunciation of Russian wasn't better. It was, after all, his mother tongue. When many years later I met his mother, who as a young woman had been a physician in Moscow, I discovered that she spoke a beautiful cultured Russian. Somehow the displacements and dislocations of Max's childhood and youth had overlaid his mother tongue with a distinctly foreign coating.

Americans tended to judge him by his English, which made him sound like a character in an ethnic comedy. He had the same guttural accent in English as in Russian and French, and moreover his English was a unique blend of GI slang and sociological jargon interwoven with bizarre inventions of his own.

Americans would stop each other in the corridors of RL and ask, eyes rolling, "Have you heard the latest Maxism?" Today, years later, I regret that I did not preserve more of Max's sayings by writing them down. At first such solecisms sounded merely funny; in time we began to see that Max had a kind of poetic inner ear. While perverting English, he also embellished it. Not long after I met him, he confided in me that there was a place in downtown Munich where you could get things "dir-r-rty cheap." He also mentioned a friend who was "vor-r-rking like a grudge."

Max once briefed a meeting of American executives on his work and startled them by explaining that he had had trouble finding the elusive answer to a problem until "suddenly it doomed on me." Now, he assured them, "I've got the matter r-r-right under my thumb tips."

Much as we liked Max and enjoyed his amusing contributions to the English language, we found it hard to take him seriously as a colleague. In addition to his communication difficulties, he had a face that bore a permanent look of puzzlement, probably the result of all the new and strange cultural experiences that he had had to confront in his life.

An acting director of RL, a sophisticated naturalized American from Romania named Lionel "Ruby" Rubinstein, always addressed Max as Slapsy Maxie, after the boxer Max Rosenbloom who played himself as a punch-drunk fighter in Hollywood movies. Ruby himself spoke half a dozen Western languages elegantly and eloquently, and had little patience with bumblers. He had operated a used-car lot in Amityville, Long Island, before getting into the international broadcasting business, and he considered himself a shrewd judge of human character. He made the diminutive Slapsy Maxie the regular butt of his jokes.

After confiding his plans to us, Max set quietly about his work, shrugging off Ruby's harassment. For a long time, there was little evidence of activity, except for his frequent out-of-town trips, causing cynics to suspect him of touring Europe at RL's expense.

In time the upper echelon at RL began to receive envelopes marked "confidential" from Max's office. Inside were audience reaction reports describing comments about listening to RL gleaned from conversations with individual Soviet citizens. Our own reaction was mixed. On the one hand, it was exciting to have this feedback, however limited. On the other hand, the reports never gave names, only cryptic references to the source like "forty-year-old Ukrainian botanist." Other details, such as the location of the interviews, were also fuzzy. Those of us who had been exposed to Soviet politics understood that naming names and places would compromise Max's sources and his whole operation, but there were skeptics who took this lack of precision as a sign that he had fabricated the reports.

Fortunately for Max, one of those who believed in him was our big boss back in New York, Howland Sargeant, who had a good appreciation of social science techniques. Sargeant, like the rest of us, had to take much of Max's work on trust. To Max the security of his interviewees was paramount, and he gave few details of his operation even to his closest friends, which served to confirm some people's suspicions. He was equally close-mouthed with the CIA, which he did not trust to protect his interviewees. Years later a CIA official complained to me, "That son of a bitch never told us anything!"

Gradually, some of us began to get a more reassuring picture of what Max was up to and how he was operating. For example, I knew a man in a Western European office who regularly met with Soviet delegations; I discovered that he was insinuating leading questions into the social chitchat, some of it tête-à-tête, that took place before and after the meetings, and then passing on to Max any references to RL or other broadcasters. No doubt his superiors would have been horrified had they known what he was doing. In this case, as in others that I knew about, no money changed hands. Max had a genius for motivating people to do things for other reasons, usually the desire to put one over on Moscow.

Max's doings came quickly to the attention of Moscow and its security people. The Soviets must have been particularly stung by an incident at the Brussels World's Fair in 1958. A high-level Soviet visitor to the fair was Politburo member Anastas Mikoyan. Accompanying Mikoyan was Ekaterina Furtseva, the heavyset minister of culture and reported mistress of Nikita Khrushchev, then at the height of his power. Mikoyan and Furtseva were introduced to a young American "student" visiting the Soviet Pavilion at the fair and insisted on having their photograph taken with him. The three appeared, arms around each other and smiling, on the front page of the daily news sheet put out by the Soviet Pavilion. It could not have taken the Soviet security people long to discover that the American student was in fact an RL staffer. "Khrushchev's girlfriend doesn't wear a girdle," the staffer told me proudly when he returned to Munich.

I found out more about Max's operation when briefly I became involved in it myself. Every two years the Kremlin and its foreign sycophants staged mammoth "world youth festivals" in various capitals. The centerpiece of such festivals was a large Soviet delegation of specially indoctrinated youths whose job was to harangue young people of other countries about the superiority of the Soviet system. To Max the presence of large groups of Soviet citizens, even "loyal" ones, was an opportunity not to be missed. He would recruit freelance interviewers to pose as "progressive" youth and engage the Soviets in conversation, then report items of interest to him.

In 1959 a World Youth Festival took place in Vienna, only a short trip from Munich. Partly to help Max and partly in order to meet some Soviets, I volunteered to work for him as a temporary interviewer. At the festival I found it easy to meet the Soviets: Max had teamed me with a languidly beautiful Russian-speaking Circassian woman named Aza who attracted young Soviets as honey attracts flies. Aza regularly wore a fresh flower in her long black braids and always looked as if she had just dressed for a party. She and I would stand in some public place casually chatting in Russian, and the young Soviets would invent some pretext to come up to us. Still, Max was dissatisfied with my performance: I was diffident about inserting RL into the conversation, preferring timidly to talk about general matters and not arouse the suspicions of my interlocutors.

The Vienna experience gave me a good look at how Max operated. We shared a hotel room, which he used for holding meetings with his interviewers. I remember being awakened early one morning because a Russian from London had sat down heavily on my feet to report on his latest chats with Soviets.

I came back to Munich utterly convinced that Ralis had a good thing going, even though this or that aspect of it might be criticized on methodological grounds. In the face of Moscow's determined efforts to prevent unstructured meetings between its people and foreigners, Max was building up a substantial body of authentic interviews with living, breathing Soviet citizens. Sargeant used these interviews to good advantage in getting government support for RL's new transmitter base in Spain, which was far more effective in reaching Soviet listeners than our weak installation in Lampertheim had been.

Max's success in Vienna led him to mount even larger operations at later youth festivals. His activities irritated the Kremlin, which began to devote extensive media space to exposing Max and his interviewers as "CIA agents." Both in propaganda and in security briefings held before their departure abroad, Soviet participants in the festivals were warned to stay away from anyone who brought up the subject of broadcasting. Some of them confided that information to Max's interviewers.

None of this deterred Ralis. After a particularly successful collection of data at the 1962 World Youth Festival in Helsinki, the Soviet media devoted months of shrill attacks to him (more attention than they gave our broadcasts). One diatribe appeared in *Izvestiya,* the official government newspaper, another in the prestigious literary journal *Friendship of the Peoples.* Ralis & Co. were described as "agents of the CIA" who "headed the delegation of provocateurs who were spreading dirty rumors and slanderous literature at the festival." To me, this was an additional sign that Max was doing something right. Slapsy Maxie was being taken very seriously by the Kremlin. (Although there is no connection, I cannot help noting that Ruby Rubinstein, who mockingly coined that name for Max, was soon back on Long Island, this time running a hotel.)

Max's data furnished important new insights into radio listening in the Soviet Union. At the same time, they failed us in one important respect: they could not tell us the actual number of listeners. In New York Sargeant was particularly embarrassed at high-level meetings because his opposite number from RFE was now tossing around figures like 55 million for the claimed size of his station's Eastern European audience. People wondered: if RL couldn't quantify its audience this way, did it have something to hide? Such questioners were apt to be unaware that Soviet society was much more opaque to outside investigation than the East European countries. Still, such ignorance was a reality to be dealt with.

It was only a matter of time before Ralis rose to this challenge, too. To step up data collection in the field, he hired a deputy, a red-bearded young Finnish-American from Minnesota named Gene Parta. Partly at my urging, they moved their operation from Munich to Paris, which was more on the beaten track for Soviet travelers and less tied to Cold War associations.

In interviewing Soviet travelers, it was essential to keep a low profile, because otherwise the governments of the countries they were visiting were apt to be pressured by the Kremlin and to crack down on Max and Parta and their teams of interviewers. The passion for secrecy was such that even colleagues and friends like me were kept away from the interviewing operation. Only years later, when I had a good business reason, was I allowed to inspect the activity. I flew to Copenhagen with an amiable young American named Charley Allen, a member of the audience research staff with an M.A. in Soviet studies from Harvard. There I stayed in the Admiralty, a marvelous hotel converted from a centuries-old waterfront building; the mammoth wooden beams of its huge skeleton had been left as they were and now passed right through the rooms, forcing guests to bow low on their way from bed to bath. The hotel was near the dock where Soviet tourist ships with hundreds of passengers berthed regularly. Shops in the area stocked cheap Western goods, often secondhand, and sported signs in Russian offering to sell their wares for rubles. Charley explained that when a Soviet ship was in, the district was thronged by passengers looking for souvenirs of their trip to the West. He said individual passengers were usually more than willing to have RL's Russian-speaking interviewers help them find bargains, and then to have a drink and a chat in a nearby cafe.

I attended a staff meeting of the local interviewing team. Most were Russian émigrés living in Copenhagen. One was an unfortunate Dane who had somehow fallen into the grip of the KGB and spent years in a Soviet concentration camp, where he learned to speak Russian fluently. Another was a Danish university professor specializing in Russian and Soviet studies. What impressed me most about the group was their genuine interest in things Russian and the delight they took in meeting Soviet citizens—forbidden fruit, as it were—and in being helpful to them in purely human terms.

In the 1960s, as the data base built up, Ralis and Parta began working quietly with a group headed by the political scientist Ithiel de Sola Pool at MIT's Center for International Studies. In time Ralis, with Parta's help, supplied the group with data from some two thousand interviews with Soviets traveling abroad. Using the interviews and other sources, Pool and his associates then came up with a computer simulation of the Soviet communications audience. The simulation relied in part on some fancy footwork by the Harvard mathematician Frederick Mosteller, who devised a technique for estimating the characteristics of "weak cells"—jargon for population groups that were "underrepresented" in the interviews. In particular, the uneducated, the rural, and the elderly did little traveling abroad. Later I discovered that similar techniques are used for estimating newspaper readership by minority teenagers in America's inner cities, where access by interviewers is also difficult.

In 1965 Pool reported on the initial results of the simulation to an academic meeting at New York University. In 1982, when the overall data base had grown to ten thousand Soviet respondents, Pool and Parta (together with a third coauthor, John C. Klensin of MIT) updated the findings. They estimated that about one-third of the Soviet adult population, some 60 million people, were "exposed to Western radio broadcasts in the course of a year." VOA, with its popular music programs, had the largest audience, about 35 million a week, with its greatest following among the lower age and education cohorts. Next came the BBC. RL took pride in the fact that its broadcasts, although heavily jammed, had nearly as many listeners as the highly effective programs of the unjammed BBC. ("Because you broadcast in all those other languages," a BBC official told me defensively during a later London visit. "Remember, we only have Russian.")

After 1980, when tension due to the war in Afghanistan led the Soviet government to resume jamming of the other broadcasters, RL increased its share, nosing out BBC and Deutsche Welle and even approaching the VOA numbers. In 1986 RL researchers estimated that their station had about 10 million listeners daily (compared to 14 million for VOA and 8 million for BBC). In all the estimates, RL showed particular strength with the better educated listeners, especially those in the age range from thirty to forty-nine, and in non-Russian areas.

The MIT simulation remained for years the backbone of RL's audience research activity and was widely accepted by people who had to make funding decisions, especially for the new Spanish transmitters. There were also skeptics. In Washington, research officials at the U.S. Information Agency (USIA), VOA's parent body, frustrated by their own office's inability to match Ralis's feat, picked at flaws: "What you have is a self-selected sample." For methodological purists, that was akin to pronouncing anathema. Max's response was a Gallic shrug, a gesture of insouciance he had learned while a French *poilu:* it would have been nice to have a neat random sample, but with the KGB on the other side that was a pipe dream. His confidence in his own work was buoyed by the fact that, as the Soviets began to use modern social science techniques to study their society, such data as they released showed a remarkable conformity to his own. In those early days, you either relied on Max's studies or went without. "Max has the only game in town," people would say, half in despair, half in admiration. I think the fact that the RL data showed larger audiences for other stations helped build confidence in the operation.

The audience estimates were only part of Max's output. He was also issuing masses of "anecdotal" information, gleaned from his interviews, on political, economic, and social attitudes and conditions in the Soviet Union. In time his product gained acceptance. Other radio broadcasters to the Soviet Union–from BBC to Deutsche Welle to Radio Sweden–began to use the Ralis data as the basis for estimating their audiences and to cite them in reports to their top managements.

Some even began to put up money toward the expense of collecting the data. The capper came some years later when USIA gave office space to one of the top RL audience researchers so that he would be on hand for consultation with its staff. Max's other information, on Soviet conditions and attitudes, came to be eagerly scanned by diplomats and political analysts in Western governments.

Much later, after the Soviet system collapsed and the former republics of the USSR became open to foreign investigators, it became apparent that the Ralis data were very close to the mark. Happily, by that time Max's technique of interviewing travelers outside the country had become an anachronism. You could go in and do your own survey, right on the ground.

I hope that future historians will recognize that, during the Cold War, Western knowledge of closed Soviet society was immensely enhanced by the vision and energy of a determined little man who spoke funny English and was once widely known as Slapsy Maxie.

Max's stature in the Western world kept on growing, but his English remained quaint. Once, years after I had left Munich and was working in RL's New York headquarters, Max and I drove up to Rockland County to have lunch with his mother, a venerable lady in her late eighties who by then had lived in the United States for more than thirty years and spoke quite passable English. At one point in the conversation Max informed her, "I just bought a suit with a west."

The old lady became agitated. "No, Max," she shouted as heads turned in the restaurant, "Vest, vest!"

The Max Ralis story has both sad and happy endings.

The sad part occurred during RL's time of troubles in the 1970s and 1980s, a period that I shall discuss later. Briefly, RL fell into the clutches of a former RFE executive who evidently had been nursing a grudge against it for years. A stolid type with strong dislikes, he seemed to many to be setting about systematically to settle scores with those who had built up RL and made it successful. Max was one of the victims. German labor law was invoked to force Max to retire at age sixty-five in 1980. Because Max was a U.S. citizen who had been hired in New York to work for an American firm overseas, it seemed to him—and many others—that the action to get rid of him under German law was grossly unfair. He sued in American court but lost the case after the new management retained a high-powered law firm, and he lost again on appeal—proceedings that ate deeply into his life's savings.

The happier part was that in retirement Max moved to the charming old French city of Orléans on the banks of the Loire, where he lives in comfortable style together with his beautiful and loving young French wife in a villa surrounded by cherry trees. Still, whenever I visit them there Max growls about being cut off from the world of Soviet (now ex-Soviet) affairs to which he once made such a memorable contribution.

A Brooklyn Window on the World

9

By the mid-1950s "Radio Hole-in-the-Head" was growing up. It had found its own voice, a voice that was telling Soviet listeners important truths about their own country, about its present and past, that they could never dream of reading in *Pravda*.

From the beginning, Ronny Ronalds, head of the News Department, was not content with this concentration on the Soviet Union's domestic affairs. He worried about how to expand listeners' vision beyond their own country. Symptomatic of the psychological isolation of Soviet citizens, even our émigré staff were mostly ignorant of and indifferent to the world outside their former homeland. Typical of our staff's lack of global sophistication was a line from a script proposed for broadcast by our Ukrainian desk: "In the words of the old Ukrainian proverb, the pen is mightier than the sword."

Wasn't RL neglecting an important opportunity to tell its audience things about the outside world that might someday be meaningful to reform elements in the USSR? With its talented staff of former Soviet citizens, Ronalds reasoned, RL could do this uniquely, from an insider's point of view.

We knew that the Voice of America was working hard to persuade Soviet listeners that Americans lived better than they did, telling them that an American worked only a few minutes to earn the price of a pair of shoes compared with a week's labor for a Russian. But to us, this materialistic approach neglected the richness and variety of American life and of Western life in general.

"Democratic education," Ronalds used to tell us, "that's what we need to give them." In other words, the idea of pluralism, of multiple ways of doing things, of more than one accepted ideology. But how to get the message across effectively? We were wary of offering our listeners just another set of propaganda sermons.

The solution to the problem showed up unexpectedly in Munich one day in the person of an amiable Brooklyn ex-GI, a Yale graduate in his early twenties, named McKinney Russell. Before joining RL in 1955 Russell had taken his army discharge in Germany, where he had served as a private, and stayed on in Kaiserslautern, up in the Rhineland, to run a peculiar institution called *Dom Druzhby* (Friendship House). A refuge for ex-Soviet, mostly Russian, "hard core" cases, Friendship House was sponsored by a U.S. organization known as American Friends of Russian Freedom, whose sources of funding were no more or less mysterious than RL's. For the slightly built McKinney, being a "friend of Russian freedom" was taxing: frequently he had to jump into his Volkswagen Beetle and rush to a police station to persuade the authorities to free an errant alcoholic or petty criminal who was in his charge, then bring the miscreant back to Friendship House and try to persuade him to behave. Two years of this had given him an enviable command of Russian thieves' slang and barracks talk, but he was ready for something else.

The first thing we noticed about McKinney when he came to Munich looking for work was his linguistic gift. He mastered languages as if they were no more complicated than the Brooklyn Dodgers lineup. Yale had standardized his English, but he could easily revert to the Brooklyn vernacular whenever someone from the borough showed up. More to the point, his Russian was extremely fluent. His German was so authentic that Germans were apt to mistake him for one of their own. Once when he was invited to a party at the home of a U.S. official, the German maid who helped him out of his coat took her employer aside and, pointing to McKinney, warned: "Be careful, that man over there pretends to be American, but he's really German." For relaxation, he would curl up with a phrase book in Finnish or Malay or Welsh. His first assignment at RL was the prosaic one of running the translation section; he and his staff translated radio scripts into English for higher-ups who could read no other language.

That assignment soon changed. In 1955 the International Confederation of Free Trade Unions (ICFTU) held its congress in Vienna. Someone—probably Ronalds—had the idea that this would be a splendid way to launch RL's democratic education. We would interview leaders of free trade unions from all over the world. If they criticized their own governments, or even the United States, so much the better: that would help to illustrate the contrast with the Soviet Union's government-controlled unions and offer a lesson in pluralism. It would also, we thought, underline an important truth: not all leading people in the West were capitalists.

Back in New York our colleagues Boris Shub and Gene Sosin had already led the way in conducting broadcast interviews with prominent people. On the eve of the 1954 Congress of Soviet Writers, the first held in twenty years, they and their staff taped conversations with American writers, such as Upton Sinclair, Thornton Wilder, John Dos Passos, James T. Farrell, and Max Eastman, as well as with Leo Tolstoy's daughter Alexandra, who had settled in the United States. Some of the interviewees urged Soviet authorities to end persecution of their writers.

For the ICFTU congress I was asked to lead an expedition to Vienna, and I asked higher authority to let McKinney go with me. It was an unforgettable adventure. To conduct day-to-day broadcasts, we took along a third person: Anatole Renning, a tall, gangling, otherworldly Estonian. Renning, who was living in exile in Sweden, had been recommended because he worked as the Swedish labor movement's expert on Soviet unions and spoke perfect Russian.

The four-power occupation of Austria was to end shortly, but in the meantime it was still very much in force. To reach Vienna our RL crew had to pass through the Soviet Zone, a risky business for all but especially for Renning, who was legally in Moscow's eyes a Soviet citizen guilty of treason, a capital crime. The only way we could travel safely was via the Mozart Express, a U.S. Army train normally reserved for government personnel that made the run from Salzburg in the American Zone. Somehow we managed to pull strings with U.S. headquarters in Munich to get the three of us on the passenger list.

The trip itself was exciting, as the train decorated with American flags crept slowly through level crossings where armed Soviet soldiers in horse-drawn carts stared stolidly at the passing imperialists, separated from us by only a pane of glass. It was somehow like an old western movie where the train passes through country peopled by hostile Indians. McKinney and I kept our noses to the window. On the other hand, Renning—the man with the price on his head—slept peacefully throughout the trip. We were discovering in him a somnolent disregard for personal danger, to the point of irresponsibility. Soon we were calling him Sleeping Jesus.

Arrival in Vienna heightened the drama. This was the city of *The Third Man,* of Orson Welles in his role as Harry Lime. I had recently seen Carol Reed's thriller, in which intelligence services played lethal tag with each other. The real Vienna was soon to compete with the film version, with our little group as players, but with overtones of farce.

When we stepped out of the Mozart Express at the Westbahnhof in the American sector, a tall redhead in an unmistakably American sport jacket walked up to us on the platform: "Is one of you guys named Critchlow?"

I told him I was.

"Well, I'm Colonel Jones, head of Army G-2, intelligence, here." He showed his identification, then waved a copy of the train's passenger manifest at me. "What the hell are you guys doing bringing a stateless Estonian to Vienna? Going to blow up the Soviet *komendatura?*"

I tried to explain to the colonel our plan to interpret the ICFTU to Soviet radio listeners. He seemed skeptical. "Well, this can be a rough town. If you have a problem, here's my card."

We checked into a room for three in a sleazy hotel near the railroad station, a typical Viennese hostelry where accommodations were rented either by the day or by the hour. From there we made our way from the American sector to the Congress Hall in the international sector. Along the route we saw jeeps patrolling the area with four-man crews, military police from each of the occupying powers. Despite the four-power security, we had heard that gangs of thugs, kidnappers working for the Soviets, roamed the international sector with impunity, grabbing anyone they wanted. If the Kremlin could order RL employees assassinated in Munich, what would it do in occupied Vienna, in its own backyard? If they found out there was a bunch from Radio Liberty in town, would they keep their hands off us? We were soon very conscious that just down the street from the Congress Hall was the beginning of the Soviet sector. There were no dividing lines; you had to know where you were.

At the Congress Hall we set up a division of labor. Renning roamed around collecting material for a daily Russian-language news report on the conference. McKinney and I had assigned ourselves the task of getting taped interviews from the union leaders present, in the form of greetings to Soviet workers that could be translated into Russian back in Munich and used for a series of future broadcasts.

Right away, McKinney impressed me with his initiative, his energy, and his ability to strike up a conversation with someone in almost any language that came along. We interviewed delegates from many countries. I remember in particular Ahmed Ben Salah of Tunisia and John Kosy Tettegah of the British Gold Coast (now Ghana), who later achieved new fame when their countries became independent. Some of the greetings were merely perfunctory, but others were thoughtful and often moving messages. The best ones expressed sincere feelings of solidarity with workers in the Soviet Union in terms of the common problems of laboring people everywhere.

No doubt because word had gotten around that RL was funded by the CIA, some of the American labor leaders were hard to approach. Victor Reuther, who handled international relations for the CIO (this was before its merger with the AFL), made it clear that he wanted nothing to do with us. In a gift shop McKinney and I cornered David Dubinsky, head of the New York–based International Ladies Garment Workers Union, and asked whether he would care to air greetings to Soviet workers. The diminutive Dubinsky, veteran of many labor wars, glared at us from among the souvenir postcards. "Greetings, shit," he growled. "My six-year-old granddaughter can give greetings. Is that the best you can do?" After unburdening himself in this way, Dubinsky gave us an interview, and a good one.

Of the dozens of interviews that we taped, our best, we agreed, came from the head of the British miners union, Sir Will Lawther. McKinney became acquainted with Sir Will first and offered to introduce me. Never having met a knight before, I shined my shoes, slicked back my hair, and showed up at the appointed time and place. There was McKinney with a pudgy, friendly man who spoke with the working-class accent of the English Midlands.

Before we could get down to business, Sir Will leaned over and whispered in my ear, "Hey, boy, where's the piss corner here?" After relieving himself, he settled down with a microphone and gave an absorbing impromptu talk to Soviet miners. He spoke straight from the heart. "Whether you're a miner in Russia or Britain or America," he began, "we all have one thing in common: mining is a dirty, dangerous business."

In the midst of all this, our responsibility for the safety of Sleeping Jesus was a constant preoccupation. He had a tendency to wander off, and until his return we never knew whether he had been snatched by the Soviets. One night at about 3 A.M. I happened to wake up and found his bed empty. I awoke McKinney, and together we bit our nails while we wondered what action to take. Before we could decide, Renning showed up looking pleased with himself. "I decided to take a walk in the Soviet Sector," he said. "It's very interesting." Renning was doing a good job with his daily radio reports, but this was hard to forgive.

McKinney and I were sitting one day in the press room of the conference when a young man walked in with a copy of the *New York Herald-Tribune* (Paris edition) tucked under his arm. His dapper suit looked Italian in cut, his haircut French. He asked in French for directions. When we answered in the same language, he inquired where we were from.

"De la Radio Liberté, à Munich," we told him.

The young man's eyes grew large. Suddenly he burst out in Russian: "My God, I never thought I'd be talking to any of you!"

I assumed that he was a Russian émigré journalist from somewhere, and asked for particulars.

"I'm from the World Peace Council in Stockholm," he told us, "a member of the Soviet staff."

In those days at the height of the Cold War, the presence of a Soviet citizen at a vehemently anti-Communist meeting was startling. To find him chatting with people from RL, even inadvertently, was all the more so. But he did not seem in a hurry to get away from us.

What followed at first was a hostile and rather silly polemic, as our Russian interlocutor challenged us to prove that the Soviet worker did not live better than his American counterpart. We wrangled on in that vein, each side using its stock arguments, until suddenly he asked point-blank, "What about the race problem in your country?"

To hell with propaganda, I thought, remembering Boris Shub's admonitions. It's time to tell the truth. "It's a national disgrace," I said to the Russian.

"And your Senator McCarthy?" he pressed me further.

"The one difference between your system and ours that I sincerely regret," I told him, "is that in our country it's not possible to have McCarthy shot."

With that his whole manner changed. He lowered his voice. "You know," he said, leaning forward confidentially, "I think your American worker probably does live better than ours. Let me introduce myself. My name is Mikhail Sergeyevich Voslensky."

After that we met several times daily with Voslensky in the canteen of the Congress Hall. We were particularly impressed by his knowedge of Western literature, much of which he had read in the original languages. For us as RL employees, it was intensely exciting to have this rare opportunity to talk to someone from "inside." (This was before the events of the last chapter, when Max Ralis made conversation with Soviet citizens a regular, if still risky, business.)

As our acquaintance progressed, Voslensky became more and more candid, and began to make scathing remarks about the Soviet system. Then he began to hint at the possibility of defecting. He said that he had always wanted to see California after reading a lyrical description of it by the French writer Simone de Beauvoir.

That particular conversation took place one rainy evening after the Congress Hall had closed. Voslensky, McKinney, and I were huddling for shelter in the doorway of a building at the border of the international and Soviet sectors, looking anxiously up and down the wet, deserted street and prepared to run for it if anyone was taking what appeared to be an unhealthy interest.

Voslensky's talk of defection made me nervous. What if it's a setup? I thought. I had read just two weeks earlier in *Stars and Stripes,* the newspaper published for U.S. military personnel, about a Soviet official in Vienna, a consular officer named Nalivaiko, who had played a sinister game with some U.S. intelligence operatives. He told the Americans that he wanted to defect, that he just needed to go to his apartment first to pick up a few things. The Americans agreed to help, and Nalivaiko asked them to meet him at a designated time in a certain cafe. While they were waiting for him there, a gang of thugs burst in whom they recognized as Soviet agents. They got away only by locking themselves in the men's toilet and climbing out a window. Were they planning the same scenario for McKinney and me? I wondered.

I remembered Colonel Jones and his card. The next morning I fished it out of my pocket and got him on the phone. "Colonel," I told him, "I think maybe we've got that problem."

The rest was like a bad spy movie.

"Go to the Bristol Hotel," the colonel instructed me. The Bristol had been taken over and was being operated by the U.S. government. "Go up to the mezzanine and stop at the second jewelry showcase on the right as you come off the stairway. Be there at ten."

Leaving McKinney to hold the fort with Sleeping Jesus, I headed for the Bristol. At 10 A.M., while I was pretending to study the jewelry in the case, I heard the colonel's voice behind me. "Don't look around," he said. "Go out the front door and turn left. The sixth car you see will have Hungarian diplomatic plates. It's unlocked. Get in the passenger's seat and wait."

I found the car, exactly as the colonel had described it. In a minute he appeared and got into the driver's seat. I began trying to tell him about our problem. "Sh-h-h," he cautioned me. "Don't talk yet."

After we had driven for some time, the colonel turned into what looked like the side of a steep hill. Young men in crewcuts, obviously American, opened a series of iron gates for us. When we were well inside this windowless redoubt, the colonel stopped the car and led me into his office.

"Okay, my boy, what's the trouble?"

I explained about Voslensky, telling him I was afraid we had bitten off more than we could chew. We were due to meet him again at three that afternoon.

"Don't worry," he said soothingly, "I'll take care of you." He pushed a button.

A young man came in, this one dressed like an Austrian. Over the years I've forgotten his name, but will call him Marvin.

"Marvin's a smart boy—he went to Harvard," the colonel introduced him proudly. "When you meet this Russian, he'll go with you and pretend to be a Viennese travel agent. If your Russian wants to go to the States, Marvin can offer to provide the ticket. His knowledge of German and the Viennese dialect is so good that no one will ever suspect he's anything but a local."

"What if Voslensky wants to meet in the Soviet sector?" I asked.

"That's all right, Marvin has friends wherever he goes."

My first shock came after Marvin and I decided to go for lunch together to fine-tune our strategy. When the waitress in the little *Kneipe* asked what we wanted to drink, Marvin ordered a beer in German but with a drawling American accent. I knew right away that it wasn't going to work, but there seemed to be no way to back out. We needed the colonel's protection.

To make a long story short, when we met in the canteen of the Congress Hall at three and I introduced Marvin as a "Viennese travel agent," Voslensky gave him a quizzical look, quickly rose from the table, and we did not see him again.

Not for about twenty years, that is, in my case. In the 1970s I was attending a convention of the American Association for the Advancement of Slavic Studies in St. Louis when I learned that the "noted Soviet historian Mikhail Voslensky" was present. Although still a Soviet citizen, Voslensky had gotten his wish to live in the West and had settled in Germany where he was affiliated with the Max Planck Institute. I sought him out, and we had a friendly drink in the bar. He had quite a story to tell.

"You know what happened to me? Obviously, someone must have found out about our meetings in Vienna, because after I returned to my office in Stockholm I was suddenly summoned to Moscow, and my passport was taken away from me."

I assured him that after our meeting in Vienna, McKinney and I had been careful never to mention his name, even to each other.

"Anyway," Voslensky continued, "I was in limbo for a couple of years. So I concentrated on my education." By the time of our meeting, Voslensky had attained not just the "candidate's degree" that corresponds to our Ph.D., but also the full Soviet doctorate accorded only to mature scholars.

I told him I was sorry about bringing in the phony travel agent back in Vienna, but that I had been nervous about the outcome of our encounters.

"I don't blame you," Voslensky grimaced, "but did you have to bring such an obvious plant? It was an insult to my intelligence."

Shortly after our St. Louis meeting, Voslensky made a splash in Western Soviet studies by publishing a book, highly anti-Communist in content, about the Soviet *nomenklatura*. He gave up his Soviet citizenship, I need hardly add.

The crescendo of our stay in Vienna, though politically an anticlimax, was a reception given for the conference participants on the last evening, hosted by the North American labor unions. It was held in the Auersperg Palace, an opulent building with many large and stately rooms that dated back to imperial times. The labor leaders showed up, most of them looking uncomfortable in suit and tie. After an initial cocktail hour at which the drinks flowed freely, we were ushered to seats amid the potted palms of the Winter Garden where an orchestra stand had been set up on the stage for dancing later on. Meanwhile, we were supposed to enjoy a soprano's rendition of German lieder.

A few Schubert songs were all this audience could take. When the soprano paused to catch her breath, I saw James C. Petrillo rush up to the orchestra stand. Petrillo, head of the American Federation of Musicians, was a household name back home in those days; he had waged a strike that kept popular music off radio and television for weeks on end. Now he grabbed a pair of maracas and began to shake them rhythmically. The leading lights of the American labor movement—then in the heyday of its power—rushed up to join him, and soon a conga line was formed, as the soprano stood disconsolately by. She never got a chance to resume. I wondered what the Soviet Communists across town would make of this manifestation of class struggle, if they could see it.

Before we left Vienna, McKinney insisted on a stroll in the Soviet sector. I was unenthusiastic. The night before, coming home from the party at the Auersperg Palace in the wee hours of the morning, I had dozed in the taxi. Suddenly I awoke and saw the Riesenrad, the giant ferris wheel of the Prater, right ahead. This, I knew from *The Third Man,* was the Soviet sector. I held my breath until the taxi reached the safety of our hotel. Now, although kidnapping was in vogue, McKinney wanted me to visit the Soviet sector voluntarily. When it became apparent that he was going to go anyway, I gave in, much against my better judgment. We parked Sleeping Jesus at the hotel and set out.

Soon we were walking through the Favoritenstrasse where the Soviet *komendatura* was located. Along the way were signs in Russian and scruffy, leather-jacketed people on the sidewalks speaking that language. We came to a small door in an opaque wooden fence that led into the *komendatura* compound.

"I'm going in there," McKinney told me. "I can't help it."

I waited out on the sidewalk, ready to sound the alarm (to whom?). After what seemed like forever, McKinney reemerged, proudly clutching a copy of *Pravda* that he had bought at an official kiosk inside.

McKinney and I both visited the Soviet Union many times in later years, but I doubt that anything ever matched the excitement of our suspenseful first encounter with Soviet power in Vienna's Favoritenstrasse, uneventful as it ultimately turned out.

The final adventure of our Vienna stay was the ride out to the international airport at Tulln in the Soviet Zone. For some reason, we were unable to return by the Mozart Express and had to take the chance of traveling through Soviet territory in a Pan-American bus with our Estonian "traitor to the homeland." Once again, nothing happened, except to my blood pressure.

McKinney's contribution to the success of our trip won him kudos in Munich. His high energy level, infectious enthusiasm, and boyish charm had enabled him to conduct many more interviews than I had. Ronny Ronalds quickly saw in him the chance to score a break-through in RL's coverage of the non-Communist world. He managed to get McKinney away from the translation section and put him to work in the News Department, where he became a roving correspon-dent, traveling all over Europe to tape interviews and roundtables with important people; the tapes were then broadcast with Russian translation superimposed. He also covered Khrushchev's famous 1959 visit to the United States for us.

Wherever McKinney went, language was seldom a problem. Once he was sent to Sweden on a two-week assignment and came back fluent in that tongue, astonishing the Swedish speakers in our Munich circle. One of his greatest coups was setting up a roundtable in Paris with a group of French intellectuals who had the reputation of being "anti-anti-Communist" and therefore not apt to want to be-come involved with a station like RL. One of them was Pierre Hervé, who had recently resigned as editor of the Communist newspaper *L'Humanité*. We reasoned that hearing people like that on a sup-posedly "fascist" radio station would make people sit up and take notice. It was what Boris Shub liked to call "the left hook."

Partly inspired by McKinney's success in Europe, the U.S. staff of Radio Liberty redoubled its efforts to interview prominent Americans for the broadcasts. Among them were Eleanor Roosevelt, former am-bassador to the Soviet Union Averell Harriman, New York's Francis Cardinal Spellman, the socialist leader Norman Thomas, and Martin Luther King. I happened to be in New York when the interview with Mrs. Roosevelt was scheduled; my friend Gene Sosin of the local staff asked me to go along with him and meet her. At her office at the United Nations, where she was then a member of the U.S. delegation, that tall, gracious lady received us warmly. But when the tape re-corder was turned on, she got right down to business, sharing with Soviet citizens her thoughts about the importance of human rights in the world.

Growth and the passage of time took their toll among the Ameri-can staff. Mild-mannered, quixotic Manning Williams, the former West Virginia journalist who was the station's first Munich director, soon began to show the strains of office. He alternated between paralysis and outbursts of ungovernable temper. Once when I showed up at a staff meeting with a cup of coffee, he threw me out bodily, growling through clenched teeth: "Damn it all, this isn't a kaffeeklatsch, it's a radio station."

Williams put on another scene one morning when Ronalds and I both happened to show up for work, Bavarian style, in leather shorts. He made it clear that if we ever did that again, we'd have to find another place to wear them.

It wasn't Manning's temper but his paralysis that finally did him in. At a morning meeting in 1955, he told the staff grimly that he was returning to the United States. Years later, when I was working directly for Howland Sargeant, the man who had fired him, I tried to find out what had happened.

"Very simple," Sargeant told me. "I wrote him a letter and I couldn't get an answer out of him. I tried and tried, but nothing happened. So we had to let him go." I never found out what was in the letter.

We had mixed feelings about Manning's departure. Most of us had grievances against him, brought on by his high-handed treatment of RL staffers. On the other hand, he understood the Soviet Union; the series of ignorant mediocrities who replaced him almost made us miss him at times. Sometimes Sargeant's actions were inscrutable, but his strategy seemed to be to give in to political pressures where he had to in the long-term interest of maintaining support for the station, even if this meant at times appointing to the RL directorship persons with dubious credentials and relying on people like Ronalds and the rest of us at the "working level" to carry on with the job.

Whatever the case, after Manning left we were no longer hobbled by his bureaucratic indecision. With Sargeant's encouragement, Manning's successors allowed us to do things pretty much our own way as far as substance was concerned, although they continually harassed us with administrative demands. But our relative freedom opened up RL to the achievements of people like Victor Frank in programming, Victor Zorza in Soviet research, Max Ralis in audience research, and McKinney Russell in reporting the world outside the Soviet Union.

In the 1950s, Ronny Ronalds won growing recognition as the natural creative and intellectual leader of the disparate horde that was our multinational staff. Barely thirty, he was promoted from heading the News Department to the newly minted job of program manager–a far cry from the sybaritic existence he had once led on the Princeton campus.

By 1962 my wife Pat and I had been in Munich for a full ten years. We were concerned that our two little girls, then six and seven, were speaking English with a German accent. Reluctantly, I informed Ronalds that the time had come for us to return to the United States. A few days later he dropped into my office.

"What would you say to going to Paris to set up an RL bureau there?"

Ronalds knew that Pat and I had a weakness for France. We had taken to going to that country whenever we could and spending our summer vacations on the Provence coast. We accepted in short order. There was a good reason for a Paris bureau and also for the one that was being set up in London, headed by Victor Frank. Ronalds thought the view from Munich smacked too much of the Cold War, that by being concentrated there we were out of the global mainstream and missing good programming possibilities.

McKinney Russell, by then a family man, also left Munich in 1962 so that he could join the foreign service of the U.S. Information Agency. When he was tested for language proficiency, the examiners certified his fluency in Russian, French, German, Italian, Swedish, and Polish. After an apprenticeship in Zaire, then in the throes of bloodshed, he was soon directing the USIA operation in the Soviet Union from his office in the U.S. Embassy in Moscow. His Soviet hosts clearly knew of his RL past, but in the interest of good relations with the United States they were discreetly silent until it was time for McKinney to leave. Then all hell broke loose, with a flaming full-page attack on his RL role in a leading Soviet newspaper. Later he directed USIA operations in other major countries, including Germany, Brazil, Spain, and China. He added Portuguese, Spanish, and Chinese to his official repertoire of languages (and might have added Lingala, a language spoken in Zaire, but the Foreign Service had no one who could test him in it). The recipient of two presidential awards and many other honors, he was appointed to the exalted personal rank of career minister and served as counselor of USIA, that agency's highest career position. Before retirement, the boy from Brooklyn ended his service with a year as diplomat-in-residence at Tufts University's

Fletcher School of Law and Public Diplomacy. But to those of us who knew him in Munich, the most important thing he ever did was to work for Radio Liberty.

The saddest story of those early RL years was that of Boris Shub, the genius who had inspired and trained so many of us. Although he came to Munich from time to time to "recharge your batteries for you," as he told us, he was spending most of his time as Sargeant's policy advisor in New York. From there he used to hector me with friendly but caustic personal letters accusing me of shirking responsibility for the real work of the station by clinging to my "beautiful research job." Eventually (because of his behind-the-scenes machinations, I suppose) I was put in charge of RL broadcasts in Russian, Ukrainian, and Belorussian. I still have one such Shubian exhortation, in which he wrote me: "Because in every organization of our great and noble age the bureaucrats outnumber the human beings by at least ten to one, it falls upon the handful who have more than shit in their veins to help the ones worth helping." Unfortunately, in his personal dealings, Boris was seldom capable of the calm tone that he always urged us to use in the broadcasts. His attitude to Sargeant, whom he accused of "dillydallying," became increasingly abrasive. Finally, he pushed the patient Sargeant too hard. Knowing that Sargeant's marriage to Myrna Loy was then breaking up, he made an impossibly and unpardonably crude comment to Howland about his fitness as a marriage partner.

Shortly after Boris's outburst, which came to light only later, we in Munich were shocked to hear that he was leaving RL. At about the same time, Boris's own marriage of many years to Libby broke up; he married his young secretary and had a son. When I visited the new family in New York during a home leave in 1962, they seemed very happy. On my return to Europe, I heard shattering news: so that he could ride horseback with his new wife, Boris had gone to a hospital for a hemorrhoid operation, was given the wrong anesthetic, and died in a coma, only fifty-two years old. At his burial, I heard, his elderly father David had to be restrained from throwing himself into the open grave.

Moscow-on-the-Seine

10

Fleshing out our operation in Paris was a step toward putting "Radio Hole-in-the-Head" on the big time, by expanding its horizons beyond the narrow Cold War focus of Munich. We wanted to bring our listeners closer to France with its beehive of unrestrained cultural activity, its democratic political life, and the French spirit of individualism. Paris was also an international symbol, the seat of UNESCO, of NATO, of important international conferences, and—in particular—of sophisticated émigré communities. Finally, it was headquarters for the powerful French Communist Party, which was just beginning to show signs of internal disarray. I was happy to be part of all this. In New York and London, my opposite numbers Gene Sosin and Victor Frank were working along the same lines, but Paris had a special cachet.

In Paris not all was serene. A reign of terror waged by opponents of Algerian independence was in full swing when the four Critchlows took up residence in August 1962. Bombings by *plastiqueurs* of the OAS (Organisation de l'Armée Secrète) were common; they often killed or maimed innocent bystanders. Four days after we moved into our apartment on quai Louis-Blériot, on the the Seine embankment in the Auteuil district near the Bois de Boulogne, terrorists set up an ambush for President de Gaulle when he was on his way to lunch with ex-president Eisenhower. The ambush was set for the avenue de Versailles, a short block over from the quai Louis-Blériot, but the terrorists were foiled when de Gaulle took our street instead, going right past our front door. "Our error cost us the success of the operation," one of the OAS ringleaders, a colonel, told interrogators before being shot by a firing squad. Two weeks later the same group riddled de Gaulle's car with machine-gun fire at another intersection. He and his wife magically escaped injury. We often saw the president's cavalcade of long black Citroen DS-19s crossing the Seine by the Pont Mirabeau underneath the windows of our fourth-floor apartment; each car holding a tall man with a large nose to baffle would-be assailants, it would speed past security police stationed at 100 meter intervals.

Sitting in those horrendous Parisian traffic jams, we would often be surrounded by a chorus of anti-Gaullists honking in unison to the beat of their war cry: "Al-gé-rie fran-çaise, Al-gé-rie fran-çaise." We ourselves were often stopped while driving by teams of grim-looking special patrols who wore distinctive white gauntlets and were noted for their toughness; it was disconcerting to have a machine-gun aimed nervously through your windshield while papers were checked. I remember reading in *Le Monde* that on a single day at the height of the crisis there were a million such *perquisitions*.

Signs of impending withdrawal of the French military from the North Atlantic Treaty Organization were already chilling relations with Washington. The United States had not yet undergone the humbling experience of Vietnam. An American colonel cried on my shoulder: "When I tell a colonel from another army to do something, he does it. But when I tell a French colonel to do something, he always wants to argue."

French recalcitrance drove the American media into a frenzy against de Gaulle, who came to be portrayed as almost another Hitler despite his commitment to democracy and what was to me a winning sense of humor. Could a real tyrant complain, as he did, of the difficulty of governing a country that had hundreds of different kinds of cheese? Amid rumors that he was in poor health, a journalist asked him at a press conference how he was feeling. In his reply, the general reduced himself to very human proportions: "Don't worry, young man. One of these days I shall not fail to die."

During our stay, the U.S. ambassador to France was one of our leading Russian specialists, Chip Bohlen. Years later, at a Soviet affairs conference in Virginia, I was reminiscing with him about the Paris scene in those days. I told him that my heart used to bleed for him when I would read in the paper that he had been called to the presidential residence in the Elysée Palace to receive from the formidable de Gaulle a protest about some U.S. action. For example, the French government used to complain about American overflights of their nuclear installation at Pierrelatte. To me, it always seemed that Bohlen was like a schoolboy summoned to be spanked by a stern master.

"Not at all. You needn't have worried about me," Bohlen told me with feeling. "The general was invariably the soul of courtesy and kindness." A far cry from the de Gaulle of the U.S. media. Although he was apt to be intransigent in the face of American demands, I always thought the general deserved more gratitude from us than he got. For one thing, when President Kennedy and other Western leaders were on the point of bowing to Soviet pressure on West Berlin, it was de Gaulle who stiffened their spines and saved the day. He gave unquestioning support during the Cuban missile crisis, pushing aside photographic evidence proffered by Kennedy's emissary, former secretary of state Dean Acheson, and telling him to assure the president of his support.

Despite tensions in the air, life in Paris was very appealing. After ten years in the trenches of the Cold War in Munich, the preoccupation of most French people with the quality of life rather than political abstractions was refreshing. Moreover, Paris had none of the reminders of wholesale World War II death and destruction to which we had been accustomed. Instead, we saw only an occasional plaque marking the place where French hostages or Resistance fighters had been shot by the Germans.

We quickly learned that, regardless of headlines, individual Americans were still quite popular with the French. Busy Parisians do little entertaining at home, but people often invited us out to their *maisons de campagne* for a country weekend. As the only American children in the local all-girl public school, our daughters were recipients of special attention from teachers intent on exercising the French *mission civilisatrice.* With that help, they quickly overcame the language barrier. Both climbed to near the top of the *classement,* the dreaded monthly rating system that seated each child according to grades.

The true French attitude toward the United States, not the one hyped by the media, was brought home to us when President Kennedy was shot. Because of the time difference, the news reached Paris at eight in the evening, just at the time of French television's major evening newscast. We watched a blank screen for ten minutes, then the rest of the evening was devoted to special programming on Kennedy's life and career. Next day in the Métro, I noticed that about half the men were wearing black neckties. A Frenchman, a stranger, politely stopped my wife on the street: "I don't know you, Madame, nor do you know me, but I must tell some American about our extreme sorrow at the death of President Kennedy."

My job involved close contact with the Russian émigré colony. Of all European countries, France had been the most hospitable to those fleeing the revolution. In Paris there were Russian churches, Russian newspapers, Russian bakeries, Russian delicatessens, Russian restaurants, and—to reap the tourist dollar—exorbitantly priced Russian nightclubs featuring "gypsy" singers and "Cossack" dancers. It was common to hear Russian spoken in the Métro. There was also a rapidly expanding Russian cemetery, at Sainte-Geneviève-des-Bois outside the city.

A few émigrés, like our Auteuil neighbors Prince Felix Yusupov and his wife, a Romanov relative, had managed to bring out sizable fortunes. Yusupov is famous as one of the assassins of the monk Rasputin; although well off by émigré standards, in his eighties he became obsessed with money, and we used to see him on French television quiz shows trying to win prizes. Others, perhaps most notably the painter Marc Chagall, had prospered in their own right, but for every celebrity there were thousands of the far less successful. Of the intellectuals, many clung precariously to the world of their own culture, managing to stay alive through the tiny fees paid by Russian publications or the handouts of fellow countrymen who were better off. It was rumored that one poverty-stricken poet, who since the collapse of Communism has achieved posthumous fame in Russia, survived when the going got tough by selling his wife's sexual favors.

Rank-and-file émigrés lived humbly by working in menial jobs as waiters, security guards, or cleaners. The Russian taxi driver had been a Paris institution for decades. At one point, nearly every second taxi driver in the city was a Russian. By the time of our arrival, that population was aging, but there was still a good chance that when you jumped into a cab the driver's accent would be unmistakable. Quite a few Russian drivers now owned their own cabs, usually long black prewar Citroen *traction-avants* with sagging lines and distinctive chevronned radiator grills, and worked on them lovingly when not behind the wheel. At lunchtime a long line of taxis would be parked along the avenue de New-York (later avenue du Président Kennedy) in front of the Rachmaninoff Conservatory while their drivers had lunch. The conservatory canteen dispensed, at reasonable prices, excellent homemade *borshch* and *pirozhki*. In deference to Russian custom, the French authorities closed their eyes to the sale of vodka; by French law, canteens were barred from selling anything stronger than wine.

In the office I had a Russian taxi driver right at my elbow. Gaito Gazdanov, whom I had known back in Munich when he was working at RL's news desk, had been reassigned to the city that was his second home and where for years he had driven a cab. He was now RL's Paris correspondent. Some financial success as a writer and then employment by RL had enabled him to retire from hacking, but it was still easy to imagine his small figure crouched behind the wheel, his habitual Gauloise hanging from his underlip beneath a large, hawk-like Ossetian nose as he glared ferociously at other drivers, with the crank of his taxi on the seat beside him to ward off *les voyous*. As a teenage volunteer of the defeated White Army he had escaped from Russia via Turkey and Bulgaria, after which he made his way to Paris and became a stevedore and a worker on the Renault assembly line before graduating to driving a cab at night. During World War II he had helped Jews and Soviet prisoners escape the Germans. He was completely at home in the Parisian environment and could bandy words in pure argot with cops, shop assistants, or cafe waiters—people who said *pif* for "nose" and *tif* for "hair" and *kif* for "drugs."

Viewing Gazdanov in that setting, one could easily forget that here was a writer whose books and other works had been translated into French, English, Spanish, and Italian. Nor could I foresee that one day he would be the subject of a Harvard Ph.D. dissertation or that many years later, after the Soviet regime had collapsed, his books would be republished in Moscow and circulate, at last, in his native country. In his novel *The Specter of Alexander Wolf,* in a passage that I took to be autobiographical, Gazdanov has his narrator confess to suffering from *razdvoenie,* a conflict between love of esthetic pleasures and the pull toward more physical outlets for his energy, such as street-fighting.

After coming to Munich to work for a few years at the news desk, where I had first met him, Gazdanov had returned to Paris for RL to cover all aspects of life that might interest Soviet listeners. We had been good friends back in Munich, where he regularly used to beat me at pool in a local tavern. Before I joined him in Paris, he was very much on his own, reporting only to Munich. Now that I was nominally his boss we remained on good terms, but on condition that I refrain from interfering too much with his work. He had the best office in our suite on the rue Cambon, one whose windows looked across a courtyard into the workroom of Coco Chanel next door, but I made no effort to dislodge him. I suspected that he spent more time in his office writing novels and short stories than doing pieces for RL, but Munich was happy with his output so I kept my peace.

We had delightful lunches in the cafés around the office or, on special occasions, in a Russian restaurant called the Praga, during which Gazdanov would regale me with stories of Paris life in general and the Russian colony in particular. Letting Georgii Ivanovich, as he was called by everyone at RL, flout my authority was a small price to pay for the pleasure of his company. He affected the tough exterior of the Parisian underclass, but his writings betrayed an extraordinary sensitivity and love of human beings. I caught only rare glimpses of that side of him, however, once when my two small daughters were brought unexpectedly to the office and his craggy, wrinkled face broke instantly into a smile of extraordinary radiance.

One of the vivid characters on the Paris Russian literary scene, a crony of Gazdanov's, was the literary critic Georgii Adamovich, a short, smiling man and charming conversationalist. Although he had been in the emigration for many years, Adamovich still had a lively reputation in the Soviet Union. When the revered Leningrad poet Anna Akhmatova was finally allowed to travel to the West in the 1960s after decades of being on the outs with the regime (which had shot her husband and imprisoned her son), she made a point of looking up Adamovich in Paris, and they had a long tête-à-tête.

Adamovich's friendship with Gazdanov persisted even though the critic had on occasion lambasted Gazdanov's writing. It happened that Adamovich had two passions other than literature: gambling and young men. Periodically he would disappear from Paris for a week or so, and we knew that he was in the Midi, dividing his time between the gambling casinos and the naval base at Toulon. During these excursions he got little sleep, causing Gazdanov to worry about his health. Once after one of Adamovich's "vacations," Gazdanov found a blunt way of expressing his concern. Over a glass in some café where the two had been drinking rather heavily, Gazdanov–who did not share his friend's sexual proclivities–blurted out: "You know, Georgii, if the French Republic had all the money that you spend on representatives of its naval forces it could build a whole new battleship!"

Despite Gazdanov's caution, Adamovich continued his routine and in time suffered a near fatal heart attack. He died after I left Paris, and I did not learn the exact circumstances of his death.

On one memorable occasion, Gazdanov and I prevailed on Munich to send my old friendly enemy Pylayev to Paris to do a series of specials. As I had learned from our earlier trip to Brussels together, Pylayev had an extraordinary gift of empathy that enabled him to bring strange scenes to life in colorful images–word pictures that could be visualized by a Soviet listener on a remote steppe who had never been far from home. At the same time, I was nervous that the fleshly temptations of Paris might make him go haywire. I need not have worried: the creative professional in him took over, and for three days he lived only for his job.

Pylayev's peasant shuffle and distinctively Soviet manner of speech (very different from that of the Paris émigrés) offended some of the Russians he came across and amused others. I had encountered the same thing when I came to Paris after ten years of hobnobbing with ex-Soviets in Munich. A Russian aristocrat said to me heatedly, "Your Russian isn't bad, but your accent is terrible."

"Well, after all," I replied defensively, "I am an American."

"But your accent isn't American, my boy, it's Soviet. You must do something about it."

With Pylayev in town, Gazdanov helped us recruit a Russian taxi driver to take us around. Pylayev with a Nagra portable tape recorder sat in the front seat next to the driver, Gazdanov and myself in back. Pylayev would compose word pictures of the passing scene into the microphone, with helpful–usually witty–interjections supplied by the driver or Gazdanov, two veterans of Paris life. In that way we recorded hours of tape as we rolled down the Champs-Elysées, along the Seine embankment past the Louvre, through the working-class districts of the Bastille and La République, up the hill to Montmartre with its superb view of Paris roofs, past the Russian cathedral in the rue Daru, into the bourgeois neighborhoods of Passy and Auteuil, then across the river to the Sorbonne and the Latin Quarter. We stopped at points of interest along the way so that Pylayev could describe the scene in detail. After midnight one night we did our taping amid the wee-hour eateries of Les Halles, then still the main market district of Paris and well known to Soviet citizens from Evgenii Evtushenko's poem "Onion Soup" and from Russian translations of Émile Zola and other writers. Next day we stood under the four mammoth cast-iron pillars of the Eiffel Tower as Pylayev, ad-libbing from notes on the back of an envelope, painted a whimsical worm's-eye view of the passenger elevators that run up the sloping pillars "like beetles climbing the legs of a spider and then disappearing into a huge iron uterus at the center."

On the eve of Pylayev's triumphal return to Munich, the fruits of his labors filling many reels of tape, our four-man team celebrated with a gala farewell dinner. I raised my glass and toasted his devotion to duty.

"Screw devotion," Pylayev snarled back at me, "get me a French girl." Again my pursuit of Russian studies took a bizarre twist, this time making me a Russian-French interpreter in a whorehouse near the rue du Faubourg Saint-Denis.

My various duties as bureau chief kept me from much direct participation in broadcasting. One of my concerns, as Franco-American relations deteriorated, was staying in the good graces of our host government. Not long after my arrival in Paris, I had a scare when the office telephone rang and a disembodied voice told me that it was calling from the Ministry of the Interior, that an investigation of my activities had been ordered. The caller demanded a meeting with me. I gulped and invited him to the office. Next day an athletic, tough-looking man in plain clothes showed up and flashed a card identifying him as Pierre Levergeois, "officier de police principal." Since it was just before lunchtime, I suggested that we have a meal together. Levergeois accepted with alacrity, and we had the first of many lunches. It seemed that on a policeman's salary he normally had to take the bus out to Orly, nearly an hour's trip but free to policemen, in order to be able to eat cheaply at home.

Levergeois soon became a kind of guardian angel to our office, dropping in from time to time to see how things were going and offering to help when we had problems with the French bureaucracy. In time we became good friends; years later he and his wife visited us when we were living in Washington. Levergeois confided to me things about his service, the DST (Défense sur le Territoire) or French counter-espionage, that probably no other American knew. He often participated in arresting suspected Soviet spies and would tell me the juicy details next day. One day he told me of an incident the night before when he was driving a suspect home after a long day of interrogation: in a rundown section of Paris they saw a man assaulting a young woman in a vacant lot, so Levergeois had the suspected spy hold his flashlight while he dealt with the miscreant. Later, he became something of a celebrity by publishing a well-reviewed book, *Les jeunes lions,* about his experiences as a young soldier during the war, and he was given a pat on the back by his superiors at the ministry, a simple French cop who had written a book. However, when he fol-

lowed up that success (after my departure from Paris) with a volume containing outspoken revelations about his counter-espionage work with the DST *(J'ai choisi la D.S.T.)* he was summarily banned from ever again setting foot in the ministry, and his career ended abruptly.

I had many bosses. My nominal superior, for esoteric bureaucratic reasons, was Robert F. Kelley, the top man in Munich, whom most of his staff affectionately called Uncle Bob behind his back. Uncle Bob seldom gave me work to do but loved to surprise me by showing up unexpectedly at the office in late morning, on days when I thought him safely back in Munich. With Irish eyes twinkling, he would drag me off to a convivial lunch. The menu of oysters and sole never varied—all to the good, except that Kelley insisted on washing them down with a sweet Vouvray that made me gag. Uncle Bob had fascinating stories to tell of his days as founder and first chief of the State Department's division for Soviet affairs, but he turned a deaf ear to suggestions that he should write his memoirs. "Bob's stubborn," Chip Bohlen told me some years later when I mentioned the subject.

Despite my formal subordination to Kelley, others laid insistent claim to my services. Ronny Ronalds, the program manager in Munich, assumed that as RL bureau chief I was working full-time on broadcasting matters. My good friend Max Ralis complained that I should be doing more to interview visiting Soviets for audience research, to the point where our relationship was temporarily strained. Ike Patch, who was now running from his New York office an innovative program to have interesting books mailed or taken to individuals in the Soviet Union, expected me to be his agent in Paris. Finally, the Institute for Study of the USSR, a research group in Munich that operated independently of RL but from the same budget, regarded me as its Paris representative; indeed, that had been the title of my predecessor in the slot before it was captured by Ronalds for RL, so he thought.

I did find time to interview some expatriate American writers for RL, people who were of special interest because they were known to Soviet audiences from Russian translations or from having their criticisms of U.S. government policies quoted, often out of context, in *Pravda* and other outlets. One was Mary McCarthy, but either she or I must have been having an off day, because all I remember of the interview is the very gracious way in which she poured tea in her Left Bank apartment, not at all like the firebrand of literary battles who once called Lillian Hellman a "Stalinist bitch."

An interview that has stayed vivid in memory is the one I conducted with the African-American writer James Baldwin the day before he flew back to the United States to take part in the 1963 civil rights march on Washington. The drama of the occasion and Baldwin's role in it had attracted world media attention, and by the time I got to him late in the day he had already done a grueling round of television interviews and was relaxing, visibly exhausted, with a glass of Scotch. He heaved a sigh of weary resignation when I pulled out my microphone. Fortunately, I still have a tape of the interview and can quote verbatim from it here. Baldwin made the point, so relevant to Soviet reality, that in some ways what persecutors do to others is not so terrible as what they do to themselves. The part Soviet listeners may have liked best was when, after discussion of the civil rights movement in the United States, I asked him whether he had something special to tell people in the Soviet Union.

> *Question:* Is there anything you could say briefly to people in the Soviet Union, anything that is valid based on the experience of this particular racial question in the United States?
>
> *Baldwin:* That's a very complex matter. I don't know the Soviet Union at all. I suppose I could ask people in the Soviet Union to bear in mind that the people of a country are always, no matter how it seems, more important than any particular government. It is a kind of triumph, no matter how bitter the record may be, that in America one is able to have the March on Washington. And what is heartening about it is precisely the fact that so many people, citizens of the country, are willing and able to make such a gesture, what is also in a way a sacrifice, to make their voices heard.
>
> The world will never be perfect and people in some ways will never change, but I think that it is a necessity, it is a responsibility of human beings as long as they are alive—insofar as they hope to become more conscious, responsible—to change their societies, to try to bring us somewhat closer to what was once called the New Jerusalem, and this transcends systems. All systems have to change and modify themselves, and they must change from within, and this is in my mind the great American hope, and it is also the hope of the world.

During my time in Paris, I experienced a kind of professional epiphany that shaped the rest of my career. A young man came into the office looking for work. He had just spent five years teaching

French in Tashkent, capital of the then Soviet republic of Uzbekistan. As I interviewed him, he began to tell me fascinating stories of life there, particularly about relations between the Uzbeks and the Russians. The picture that emerged was one of the Muslim Uzbeks slyly turning the tables on their Russian masters. I really sat up and took notice when my visitor told me, almost casually, "The Russians are going to have to get out of there, you know, it's only a matter of time."

This was very different from the picture of Soviet reality that most people then had. Like so many other Sovietologists, I had felt that the Soviet Union and Russia were virtually indistinguishable, that Russians ran the country and the other nationalities were a historical remnant rapidly losing their separate identity, given the pressures of russification. In Munich I had worked and socialized, even played volleyball, with Tatars, Ukrainians, Uzbeks, Armenians, Kazaks, Azeris, and people of many other ethnic origins, but it had never occurred to me, much as I liked some of them, to take them seriously as a political force. This chance encounter with the young man in Paris changed all that.

I went to a specialty bookshop to buy an Uzbek grammar and dictionary. At first it was only a hobby, but as the years went by I began to publish an occasional article about Uzbekistan and found myself being invited to academic conferences.

In Paris two other people helped to raise my awareness of the Soviet Union's non-Russian periphery. Noë Tsintsadze had been minister of education in Georgia, in one of the three independent Transcaucasian governments that had existed briefly after the collapse of tsarist Russia until the region was overrun by Bolshevik troops in 1921. Tsintsadze escaped to France, where he became wealthy in the yogurt business. I knew him as a feisty but lovable old man who would appear, always unannounced, at the door of my office and demand to see me. His first words, in Russian with an indescribable Georgian accent, were always the same: "You Americans don't understand a thing!" Then he would proceed to harangue me about the evils of Communism in general and the Soviet empire in particular.

Jehun Bey Hajibeyli had been a member of neighboring Transcaucasian state Azerbaijan's delegation to the Versailles Peace Conference after World War I and had lived in France ever since. A tall man of extraordinary dignity, Hajibeyli was a natural leader of his country's emigration. He was also a regular visitor to the office. Both he and Tsintsadze were willing to discuss politics by the hour, if my time permitted. I am grateful to them for having helped me to understand the potential of non-Russian opposition to Soviet power.

Hajibeyli happened to be the brother of the noted Soviet composer Uzeir Gadzhibekov, as he is known under the Russian form of the family name. I often wondered how it was possible for Gadzhibekov, the brother of a man branded a "traitor," to be continually heaped with high Soviet honors. Many years later, when I was visiting the USSR, someone told me the story of how it had come about.

It seems that Stalin had attended a performance of Gadzhibekov's popular musical comedy, *Arshin mal alan,* and enjoyed himself immensely. Afterward, he asked one of his aides whether Gadzhibekov was a party member and was told that he was not.

"Well, have him join, then," Stalin told the aide.

"But, Comrade Stalin, his brother is a renegade who lives in the West," the aide replied.

"I said, have him join the Party," Stalin said. That ended the discussion, and Gadzhibekov was taken into the party. It happened in 1938, at the height of the purges.

There was one other significant demand on my time. Soon after my arrival in Paris, Howland Sargeant dropped in from New York on his way to Munich and made it clear that he, too, had a claim on my services. Ever conscious of public relations, Sargeant saw Paris as a good place to build U.S. support for RL. He gave me a whole menu of "targets": Ambassador Bohlen and his foreign service staff; the American political advisor at SHAPE, the Supreme Headquarters Allied Powers Europe (a job then held by State Department Soviet specialist Walter Stoessel, later ambassador in Moscow); the American press corps (people like Cy Sulzberger of the *New York Times*); and the scores of influential Americans who liked to make Paris a stopover when they went abroad.

Looking back, I think that Sargeant may already have had a premonition of the very difficult, almost fatal, challenge that RL would be facing in a few years, one that would demand every scrap of support in the United States that we could muster. At the time I resented having to reduce my involvement in the foreign context after all the time and effort I had put into learning to function in it. Besides, I was having too good a time moving in the French and Russian worlds to want to spend my days with people from back home.

Exceptions were a few old Russia hands among Americans in the Paris press corps whom I found interesting. One who stands out was

Serge Fliegers. Fliegers was a colorful character who spoke many languages, including Russian. As European correspondent of the Hearst newspapers, he had to be extremely versatile, peering through a Roman hotel transom at a movie star's love nest one day, then turning out an informed and sensitive think piece on Soviet politics the next. Fliegers had panache: he lived at the Ritz and sported a jaunty waxed mustache with turned-up ends that made him look not unlike the famous artist Salvador Dali, whose face was well known to the public from his craving for publicity. Sometimes they would run into each other in the Ritz bar, a favorite hangout of Dali's.

Among Fliegers's duties was providing support for visiting Hearst executives whenever they came to Paris. One day the editor of a Hearst paper from Kansas called and said he'd like to see him.

"Sure," Fliegers told the editor, "meet me at the Ritz bar at six."

"But, Mr. Fliegers, we've never met," the editor said. "How will I recognize you?"

"That's easy," Fliegers replied. "I have a waxed mustache with turned-up ends."

At the appointed time, the editor found a man in the bar with a turned-up mustache and walked over to him. "Hello, Mr. Fliegers," he said.

The man reared back his head and looked at the editor with bulging eyes. "I'll have you know, sir, that I am Salvador Dali."

The editor did a double take. "What did you say your last name was, Salvador?"

One of my press contacts turned into an embarrassing fizzle. Pat McGrady had been Moscow bureau chief of *Newsweek* and was freelancing for a time in Paris, looking for stories that would bolster his reputation. One day in 1964 he called me and said he had a hot tip that Khrushchev was about to be thrown out as the top Soviet leader.

"Don't touch it," I advised him. "I have reason to believe it's phony."

Two days later the world was startled by news from Moscow that Khrushchev was out. Given the circumstances, McGrady was quite gracious about my making him lose the journalistic coup of the year.

Except for a few such interesting journalistic contacts, I was turned off by public relations. My wife and I dutifully went to a few American cocktail parties when we could not avoid them and were mostly bored by the small talk. Besides, being a public relations flack did not seem like the best use of whatever skills I possessed.

But Sargeant was president of the organization, and his wishes could scarcely be overlooked.

From beyond the grave, Buffalo Bill Cody helped me out of this dilemma by sending me his grandnephew Morrill. Because of his illustrious ancestor, Morrill Cody was always called either Buffalo Bill or plain Bill. He had just retired as an American diplomat and decided to live in Paris, where he had spent many happy years as a child and young man. He had come back later as cultural attaché of the U.S. Embassy and was on close terms with a constellation of writers, artists, and politicians. He spoke fluent French with a wonderfully earthy Parisian accent. When he arrived back in town after retiring, I snapped him up as a consultant. Although twenty years older than I and formerly much senior in rank, he always pretended to respect my authority. He gave the office a sparkling new dimension, both by contributing to public relations and by helping all the different elements of the RL organization that needed contacts in Paris. We became practically inseparable.

Probably because of Bill Cody's good efforts in my behalf, Sargeant became so impressed that he offered me a job in New York as director of information on his own staff, a substantial promotion, which I accepted. Before leaving, I tipped off Ronny Ronalds in Munich, where troubles with a particularly inept and overbearing RL director had begun to take a toll on his health. Between us we managed to have Ronalds appointed as my replacement. He stayed in Paris for only a year before being recruited by the Lyndon Johnson White House to go to Washington as program director of VOA.

Very reluctantly in September 1965, after three memorable years as Parisians, we Critchlows pulled up stakes, drove to Cherbourg in our Peugeot station wagon, and boarded the *Queen Elizabeth* for the United States.

Moscow-in-Manhattan  11

At the beginning of the seventeenth century, Russia underwent a period of upheaval and turmoil that historians call the Smuta, the "Time of Troubles." Toward the end of the 1960s Radio Liberty started through a Smuta of its own.

At first all was serene. After the Cold War excitements of Munich and the exhilarations of Paris, the New York headquarters of the Radio Liberty Committee, RL's corporate superstructure, seemed to me strangely quiet, even apathetic. Our floor at 30 East 42nd Street, the old Union Carbide building, looked like any other office. The staff lived like typical New York office workers, coming in by train from the suburbs or by subway from the boroughs, then going home after work to attend PTA meetings or watch *The Man from UNCLE*. Only the occasional sound of Russian or Ukrainian or Tatar in the halls was the tip-off that this was not your usual New York office.

In my new position as director of information, I was under the thumb of the committee president, Howland Sargeant, who demonstrated his keen interest in public relations by putting me in an office right next to his own. I discovered that until my arrival the committee's public relations effort had been aimed largely at getting RL's name into the papers. The publicity staff would look through the Munich research output for something that could be sensationalized for the daily media, then mail out hundreds of copies of news releases with screamer headlines. Judging from the paucity of mentions retrieved by our clipping service, most editors treated these as junk mail and threw them directly into the wastebasket, probably unopened.

To get my feet on the ground in the new job, I had a series of meetings with Abe Schecter, a savvy, crusty Madison Avenue public relations pro. One of Abe's claims to fame was that many years earlier when working for NBC he had hired a man named Lowell Thomas, who for decades reigned as America's premier newscaster. Abe's firm had been retained by RL a few years before my arrival, but much of his advice had been disregarded. Abe told me bluntly that getting RL into the papers might be good for the egos of the staff, since they could then show the item to their family and friends, but that it did little to advance RL's real interests. His advice was to focus on key groups that might be of genuine use to RL and concentrate on reaching them. It was not hard to identify the groups: government officials, scholars, and journalists, with special reference to people within those groups who specialized in Soviet affairs.

"Even if you do get RL into the papers, people forget about it the next day," Schecter told me. "Shit, I'd like to have the money RL's been wasting on those cockamamie news releases. Cut them out, and you can save hundreds in postage. And you can save thousands by firing me, because you don't really need me."

So I fired him, gratefully.

With Sargeant's blessing, I began a regular shuttle run to Washington to call on officials who were Soviet affairs specialists, mostly in the State Department and the U.S. Information Agency. We omitted the CIA, which had its own sources of information about RL. After 1966 one of my key contacts was my old Munich chum Ronny Ronalds, now at Voice of America. John Chancellor, who had temporarily left NBC at President Johnson's request to become director of VOA, had persuaded Ronalds to join him as program director, with responsibility for nearly forty languages. Unlike many Washington bureaucrats, Ronalds was not obsessed by notions of turf. He saw no contradiction between loyal service to his new employer and extending a helping hand to his old one, RL. In the critical years to come, Ronalds used his position and influence to aid us in significant ways. His work at VOA did not suffer: after Chancellor returned to NBC, two successive VOA directors, John Charles Daly and Kenneth Giddens, held him over as their program director.

The point of my calls on Washington officials was to answer any questions they might have about what RL was doing and to listen attentively to whatever advice they might give us. We also kicked around the latest developments in the Soviet Union. Sometimes Sargeant and other staff members would come down from New York, and I would organize a reception with drinks and food, at which there would be wide-ranging discussion of Soviet affairs. Attendance at those events was always very good. People left them, I am sure, with the feeling that those running RL were more than just bureaucratic marionettes whose strings were pulled by the CIA.

We had a special interest in scholars as sources of information and insight who could help us do our job better. It was important to build bridges to the academic community. I began sending copies of the best of the Munich research output to a select list of scholars. From this they could see that RL was not the sinister Cold War propaganda mouthpiece portrayed in the Soviet newspapers they read. This service caught on, and in time RL was sending its research to hundreds of academics—a practice that continued for many years, eventually on a paying basis.

As for the media, I followed Schecter's advice that we forget publicity as a priority. Instead, I concentrated on making sure that key editorial people knew something about RL in case a news story should cross their desk mentioning us. Occasionally, my colleague Ike Patch would set up a lunch for me with his old friend Harrison Salisbury of the *New York Times,* whom he had known since his Moscow embassy days during World War II. Harrison liked to go to the Russian Tea Room on Wednesdays, when they served Siberian *pel'meni.* I never told him how in my Munich days I had once been ordered not to use his stuff, and how I had obeyed the order. Gene Sosin, RL's New York bureau chief, and I often met with Harry Schwartz of the *Times* editorial board, the paper's resident Soviet specialist, who liked Chinese food. There were many others. One unforgettable contact was Paul Wohl of the *Christian Science Monitor,* an elderly man who lived in a Greenwich Village apartment with seventy turtles. Another regular on our list was John Scott of Time-Life, who had a special interest in Soviet affairs from having worked during the 1930s as a welder in Magnitogorsk, where he married a Russian woman. I doubt that any of these people were ignorant of our CIA ties, but as friends they were mostly too polite to rub it in.

Other journalists were more aggressive. That was the downside of my new job. In Munich and Paris it had been largely possible for me to go about my work without thinking about the CIA. Now, as director of information, I had to answer the perennial questions: "Where does your money come from?" or "Do you get funding from the CIA?" I quickly decided that the only possible policy was not to lie about it. Instead of denying CIA funding, I would simply reply to queries by saying that I was in no position to discuss our sources of financing. When they saw that I would not budge from this position, even in the face of the severe browbeating at which the Fourth Estate excels, reporters usually lost interest.

With few exceptions, journalists could not be bothered to look further into the RL story. Were we damaging U.S. interests or the cause of peace by broadcasting incendiary material to the Soviet Union? I would offer to provide copies of any or all programs, but never had a taker. Most reporters liked to get their news the easy way, from handouts or, as H. Ross Perot says, by playing "gotcha."

The atmosphere of foreboding about impending revelations of RL's CIA connection and the complications that they could cause was lightened by occasional elements of comic relief. In addition to journalists, I tried to maintain contacts with others who had a special interest in Soviet affairs. One offbeat acquaintance, recommended to me by John Scott of Time-Life, was Earl Browder. In my youth Browder, a former labor organizer in the Kansas City stockyards, had been the head of the U.S. Communist Party; in those days I used to see newspaper pictures of him as a stalwart Stalinist militant with a toothbrush mustache like Hitler's. To many Americans, he was then as big a menace as Hitler. By the time I met him, he was a decrepit old man who had long since broken with Moscow. It was interesting to hear him talk about relations between Moscow and the American Communist Party, and we lunched together a few times.

One day something happened that in the critical years ahead added materially to RL's domestic political muscle. I had a visit from a man named Uldis Grava, the leader of a Latvian-American association. Grava proposed on behalf of the Baltic community in the United States that RL begin broadcasting in Latvian, Lithuanian, and Estonian. For years, he told me, similar requests to Radio Free Europe had been routinely rebuffed (because, as someone at RFE later confided in me, the management feared that the astute and powerful Baltic lobby might be too difficult to handle). Now, Grava told me, the Balts were turning in desperation to RL. They had not done so before, he explained, because some of the émigrés thought that any relationship with a radio station that broadcast to the Soviet Union might be taken as de facto recognition of the USSR's annexation of their republics. Now they were ready to compromise on that point.

My after-hours research on another Soviet republic, Uzbekistan, had given me a new appreciation of the political potential of the Soviet nationalities that helped to dispose me favorably toward the Baltic request. Besides, the present policy seemed highly unjust, and

Grava inspired confidence as a reasonable and responsible partner. I told him I would look into it.

Clearly, this was the kind of decision for which we would need government sanction. With Sargeant's blessing, I called Deputy Assistant Secretary of State Richard T. Davies in Washington, the State Department's top official for Soviet and Eastern European affairs and a friend whom I knew to be one of the more intellectual and open-minded foreign service officers.

"Dick," I asked him, "if the U.S. government were to decide to support the idea of RL broadcasts in the Baltic languages, who would have to make the decision?"

Davies thought for a minute. "I guess I would," he answered. "So will you?"

He thought another minute. "Yes, by golly, I will."

I called in the Balts and explained that we accepted the principle that RL should broadcast in their languages, but that it would take time to get money through the budget cycle and that there were people along the way who might veto the project on financial grounds. Would they work with us on that basis? I asked.

The answer was a statesmanlike yes. From then on, the influential Balts, who had every reason to resent their past treatment by RFE, became our staunchest allies.

Sooner or later the CIA story had to break. In 1967, with antigovernment feeling running high in some circles because of the Vietnam War, a magazine called *Ramparts* did a series on that agency that exposed its covert funding of the National Student Association. RL was not mentioned, but our whole office trembled when a *Ramparts* reporter called to set up an interview, evidently to do a follow-up that would focus on us. As he came down the hall to my office, people peeked nervously from behind doors to catch a glimpse of this nemesis. The reporter was actually a mild-mannered young man with red hair who seemed to fear for his life—stories of CIA assassinations had begun to surface—and barely listened to my answers to his questions before dashing out of the office. The *Ramparts* follow-up never appeared. I never learned why.

The CIA story grew more serious when the *New York Times* ran a series of exposés. Popular indignation focused mainly on CIA intrusions into the fabric of American life, as in the agency's infiltration of the National Student Association, but we were caught in the backwash by a mention of RL as one of the so-called "CIA proprietaries."

As the news media scrambled to exploit the story, a wire service editor remembered a letter he had received years earlier from my predecessor, flatly denying any CIA funding of RL, and sent it around to his clients with a caustic note. Still, we were in better shape than RFE, which for years had been pretending to derive its sole support from the pennies of American schoolchildren and other private donations.

Typical of the spirit of the times was a chapter on American foreign radio that appeared in 1970 in a three-volume history of U.S. broadcasting published by Eric Barnouw of Columbia University's School of the Arts. The chapter title telegraphed the writer's frame of reference: "The Image Empire." He depicted RL as the personal tool of the "Dulles Duo," the two brothers who were appointed under Eisenhower as secretary of state and director of central intelligence. In particular, Secretary of State John Foster Dulles was portrayed as "a skillful manipulator of news and a constant broadcaster." To someone who had handled day-to-day broadcast output in Munich, this was a bizarre view of RL. At least Barnouw did take the trouble to look through some English translations of the broadcasts, but he concluded that the writers were "faithfully following an official line." Still, the broadcasts must have had some impact on him, because he summed up: "Whatever on Radio Liberty is true and fine—and apparently there is much—could be done by the Voice of America; whatever is not had better not be done."

In the aftermath of all the revelations about CIA activities, the CIA was ordered by the Johnson White House to cease funding of U.S. "private voluntary" organizations. For a time, this injunction was interpreted as applying to RFE and RL. From a knowledgeable fellow employee, I heard a story that a man had flown up from Washington one day with a black satchel. He met one of RL's fiscal executives in a bank vault, opened up the satchel, and handed our man $18 million. In those days, that amounted to about eighteen months' expenses. We were told that when the money ran out we would have to find new sources of funding.

With RFE and RL in financial limbo, the Soviets saved the day for us by invading Czechoslovakia in August 1968. This caused the government to reexamine its termination policy. It was decided that RL and RFE, which were organized to aim their broadcasts overseas exclusively, were different from American "private voluntary" organizations like the National Student Association, and "covert" funding was resumed, although by now it was hardly covert. From then on, we were fair game.

Ironically, this was at a time when RL's role and effectiveness as a broadcaster were manifestly on the rise, thanks to the flood of *samizdat* documents that had begun to circulate among dissidents in the Soviet Union and were seeping out to the West. Since copying facilities in that country were rigidly controlled, the documents had to be painstakingly retyped with multiple carbons before being passed around. There was a joke going around Moscow about a high Communist official who finds his wife busily typing away on a long document.

"What's that you're typing?" he asks her.

"It's *Anna Karenina.*"

"But why the hell are you typing *Anna Karenina?* You can buy it in a bookstore."

"I know," the wife tells her husband, "but the only way our daughter will read it is if she thinks it's *samizdat.*"

The rise of the *samizdat* movement coincided with the Moscow trial of two writers, Andrei Sinyavsky and Yulii Daniel', who were sentenced to terms at hard labor for smuggling their work to the West for pseudonymous publication. Ronny Ronalds, while still in Paris as my successor, had obtained a bootleg copy of the trial proceedings and passed it to our colleagues in Munich to be broadcast back to the Soviet Union. He also gave a copy to Henry Tanner, then the Paris correspondent of the *New York Times.* When the document appeared in the *Times,* it made a major splash. *Samizdat* became a regular component of RL programs, which meant that for the first time many of them were now originating inside the Soviet Union, bringing the radio even closer to the audience. VOA also carried *samizdat,* but on a much smaller scale so as not to involve the U.S. government too directly in the Soviet dissident movement. That left it up to RL.

RL was shaken when, in January 1971, Senator Clifford Case of New Jersey, a Republican member of the Foreign Relations Committee, made a speech on the Senate floor condemning the CIA's clandestine support of RFE and RL. He introduced a bill calling for RL and RFE to be placed directly under the secretary of state. Given the State Department's institutional aversion to any open involvement with us, the Case bill looked like the kiss of death. Later, after getting the raspberry from some of his ethnic constituency back home in New Jersey, Case gave assurances that his move was aimed not against RFE and RL but at the government's method of funding them, which he considered an anachronism now that the Cold War seemed to be subsiding.

Whatever Case's intentions, his speech was closely followed by an attack from an even more formidable quarter: Senator J. William Fulbright, the powerful Arkansas Democrat who chaired the Foreign Relations Committee.

The Fulbright Flap

12

W hen Senator J. William Fulbright spoke out against Radio Free Europe and Radio Liberty in 1971, he was much blunter than his colleague Clifford Case. He made no secret of his hostility to the stations themselves or of his desire to see them done away with, although he appeared to have little direct knowledge of them.

At the time, as we braced ourselves for further onslaughts from Fulbright, we did not understand fully the depth of his antagonism or the reasons for it. Those reasons eventually came to light, but only after the battle was over.

As I became involved in various activities aimed at defeating Fulbright's campaign against RFE and RL, it saddened me to think that our chief opponent was a man who had done good things for his country. As a freshman representative in 1943, he had achieved national celebrity through the "Fulbright Resolution," overwhelmingly adopted by the House, which provided impetus for the future United Nations. John F. Kennedy called it "the classic modern example of beating swords into plowshares."[1] However heated our struggle for survival against Fulbright, I was one of those countless Americans who would always remember him gratefully as the architect of the "Fulbright exchanges," which have contributed so much to international understanding. He also deserves credit for taking an early stand against the character assassinations of Senator Joseph McCarthy, at a time when to do so required considerable political bravery.

These were things that had happened near the beginning of Fulbright's congressional career. By 1971, when he first attacked RFE and RL, he was becoming increasingly isolated from the mainstream of U.S. foreign policy, to all appearances an embittered man.

Before I left Paris in 1965, Fulbright and his wife, then visiting the city, had been on the list of guests whom Bill Cody and I had invited to a reception at the Hotel Crillon for Howland Sargeant. Thanks in large part to Cody's reputation, I think, Ambassador Bohlen and several American and French celebrities showed up. The following day, Cody had a friendly note from Mrs. Fulbright regretting that she and her husband were caught in traffic and unable to attend in time. I used to wonder whether, if Fulbright had been able to come and talk to us and the other guests, he might not have gained a different idea of what RL was all about. Probably not, because the evidence of his speeches and writings suggests that he already had a closed mind on the issue. Later, as his attacks on us brought distinguished Americans of all political stripes to our defense—including former Fulbright scholars—he may have realized that somewhere along the line he had miscalculated in dismissing us as crude propaganda instruments of the CIA. If so, he never admitted it.

When Fulbright first began to attack RFE and RL, some of us assumed that the whole thing must be a gigantic misunderstanding, that someone had been feeding the senator false information. We assumed that this champion of international understanding would not turn his back on the many people in the Soviet Union who were dependent on RL for information, as evidenced by the organic relationship between the broadcasts and the *samizdat* movement. We didn't know how naive we were.

One of Fulbright's initial salvos was a request to the Library of Congress to investigate us and provide him with a detailed report. He evidently reasoned that exposure to the light would be our undoing.

Up in New York, we were understandably nervous as we awaited the first visit from the Library of Congress researcher assigned to look into RL. The person who showed up was a tall, scholarly, convivial Irishman named Joseph G. Whelan who had reassuring credentials: a Ph.D. in history and years of expertise in Soviet foreign policy. Whelan asked us questions for about two hours and listened carefully to our answers. Gene Sosin and I told him about the early days of RL and how the genius and influence of the late Boris Shub continued to be reflected in the broadcasts. When we finished, Whelan burst out: "You fellows aren't selling propaganda! You're selling Jeffersonian democracy!"

That encouraged us, naturally, but the next phase of Whelan's assignment was a trip to Munich to take a closer look at RL. He was accompanied by his colleague James Price, the researcher assigned to do the report on RFE.

During the Fulbright flap, I stayed closely in touch with RFE's New York headquarters, instructed to do so by Sargeant. I met often with Gene Mater, their pipe-smoking vice president for corporate affairs. Mater had been a rough-and-tumble reporter for the defunct *New York World-Telegram*. Later he was hired by RFE to run the newsroom in Munich, where he established a reputation for rock-ribbed accuracy and integrity that at times seemed excessive to his colleagues. In New York he quickly earned my respect as a gruff but decent, able, and energetic professional, and we worked smoothly together. I was saddened when he left to become a vice president of the CBS Broadcast Group, no doubt at a much higher salary. To cheer me up, Mater took me to lunch at a very expensive restaurant on his new CBS expense account, then walked me through the elegant displays of nearby Bergdorf-Goodman's ground floor. "I just wanted you to see what you're missing, Jim," he told me with a chuckle.

I found the other RFE brass uninspiring. They whined that Senator Fulbright was a government problem and that the government should bail them out. Their attitude contrasted with Sargeant's view that to stay alive, we had to help ourselves and work hard at it. The RFE staff tended to wallow in self-pity, with little action. I complained about their attitude to Sargeant and suggested that maybe we would be better off going it alone. Sargeant, a New Bedford native, gave me some nautical advice: "Jim, we're in the same boat. Don't think you're better off because it's the other fellow's end of the boat that's sinking."

We waited anxiously for the Library of Congress report to be completed. Under pressure from all concerned, the two researchers produced first drafts without delay. On our undertaking not to quote from them until they were released officially they were shown to us for comment, a routine procedure. We heaved a sigh of relief. The findings on RL were balanced and did not overlook some of our weaknesses, such as the problem of rejuvenating aging staff, but the overall picture that emerged was very positive. Confirming his initial impression, Whelan wrote that RL's "philosophical orientation, reformist, idealistic, and pacifistic, is in the tradition of American Jeffersonian-Wilsonian democratic liberalism." He summed up by writing, "In brief, RL acts as a responsible instrumentality of the U.S. Government and operates within a larger and generally acceptable consensus of American national interests."

That made us look not at all the ogre that Fulbright had evidently imagined. Jim Price's parallel report on RFE was similarly upbeat. In addition, Fulbright had asked the General Accounting Office–the congressional watchdog–to investigate the management practices of RFE and RL; it, too, was favorable.

This ought to make Senator Fulbright see the light, we told ourselves joyfully . . .

Instead, Fulbright sat on the reports. Weeks went by.

Under pressure from the White House, the top echelon of the State Department decided on steps to help us discreetly within the government. David M. Abshire, the assistant secretary for congressional affairs, was assigned to defend our interests on Capitol Hill by getting us a new legislative lease on life. The new policy opened the way for our genuine well-wishers in the foreign service ranks, people like Richard Davies, to work openly to help us. It led to designation of John Baker, an old Moscow and Prague hand who worked for Davies as head of the State Department's East Europe office, to coordinate the effort to save RFE and RL. I had known Baker as a friend ever since he had served in Germany in the 1950s and had a high regard for his dedication and integrity.

John called me at home one weekend from his office. "Jim, I've got Abbott Washburn sitting here with me. He's going to try to form a 'Citizens Committee' to support the Radios." Washburn was a respected Washington operator who had been deputy director of the U.S. Information Agency. His involvement was good news, and eventually the Citizens Committee recruited a host of distinguished Americans to our side, playing a major role in our salvation.

The trouble with such long-term approaches was that the patient might be dead before the cure could take effect. Our only hope for survival was that the government would quickly find some overt way to maintain our funding. Obviously, that would involve congressional action, with Fulbright the key player. So his refusal to release the Library of Congress reports was ominous.

Fulbright's strategy, it became obvious, was to drag his feet: knowing that the money was running out, he understood that time was on his side. Our CIA funding would be exhausted at the end of the 1971 fiscal year on June 30, and there was no question of its ever being resumed. We maintained a precarious existence under a stopgap "continuing resolution" by Congress, but that was no solution. By February 1972, eight months into the new fiscal year, Fulbright was still refusing to cooperate with congressional efforts to keep us alive, saying that Congress must see the Library of Congress report (on which he was sitting). The continuing resolution was to expire on February 22, with no hope of extension. Up in New York, the staffs were working on liquidation plans.

For one thing, we couldn't just stay on the air until the money ran out. If we closed down, there would be substantial liquidation costs, such as severance pay for employees and disposal of equipment and other assets. We had to time our closing to leave enough money to pay for it.

"You know," Sargeant told me one day, "if we wind up in the red I could go to jail." When you are responsible for disbursement of government money, you can't just file for bankruptcy.

During this desperate period, there were a few bright spots. A mutual friend put me in touch with John Roche, an old-time liberal who was then teaching at Brandeis University. (Later he became dean of the Fletcher School of Law and Public Diplomacy at Tufts.) Roche also wrote a nationally syndicated newspaper column. He came to our office on his next visit to New York and listened to our tale of woe. It was just before lunchtime.

"Give me a room with a typewriter and a ham sandwich," he asked. We gladly complied. Less than an hour later Roche emerged and handed me some sheets of paper.

"Would you mind having this delivered to King Features?" he asked. It was a column about RFE and RL. It appeared in many newspapers, including the local one we read up in Westchester. I was impressed by the elegance with which Roche, off the top of his head, had quoted Aristotle against Fulbright.

Such expressions of support were heartwarming, but the threat of our imminent demise persisted.

With Fulbright still bottling up the Library of Congress reports, I decided on desperate action. A young freshman representative from Connecticut, a Republican named Bob Steele, had once told me casually that he would like to help RL in any way he could. In college Steele had studied Russian, which gave him a special interest in our operation. After graduation, he had served briefly with the CIA before returning to Connecticut and the insurance business.

I called one of Steele's aides and explained our plight. Would the representative be willing to make a speech in our behalf? In short order the answer came back: not only was Steele willing, but he was due to speak on the House floor that afternoon. Could we supply a text right away for inclusion in his remarks?

In my New York office, I sat down and ground out six pages of text, with someone standing by to fax them to Washington, one by one (an early use of fax technology). I'm afraid the text was rather demagogical. Instead of just calling attention to the harm being done to RFE and RL by Fulbright's failure to release the reports, it took him to task for sitting on documents that had cost thousands of tax-payer dollars. Still, Steele gave the speech verbatim, his staff informed me on an open telephone line while he was speaking, and the text appeared in the *Congressional Record.*

Steele's speech stung Fulbright into quick response. Although in a statement on the Senate floor he dismissed the Library of Congress reports on RL and RFE as "two rather dreary commentaries on two very bureaucratic organizations," he had both parts published in full in the *Congressional Record.* I suspect he reasoned that few journalists would have the energy or patience to go through so many pages of fine print. But now that the reports were out, we were free to call attention to key sections of them.

Bob Steele had helped us mightily, but his action got him into hot water with the congressional leadership. Even members of his own party were critical of a freshman representative who would attack the veteran chairman of the powerful Senate Foreign Relations Committee. His first term in Congress was also his last; I never found out whether his anti-Fulbright speech was a factor.

Despite the favorable reports by the Library of Congress and the General Accounting Office, Fulbright insisted that "the Radios should be given an opportunity to take their rightful place in the graveyard of cold war relics." He muttered some unkind things about Representative Steele's old CIA connection and also about the fact that Jim Price had once written for that agency—facts that neither man had tried to conceal.

In the face of Fulbright's campaign against RFE and RL, public support for them began to grow. The well-organized Polish-American community was disturbed about the fate of RFE. In RL's corner, we had 2 million Ukrainian-Americans. Among our most effective supporters, despite their past treatment by RFE, were our new friends, the Baltic-American groups. (When the dust settled, they were broadcasting on RL.) From nearly every state, university professors, many of them regular users of the research output of RFE and RL, began to write letters to their senators and representatives. Concerned citizens in many walks of life also registered support for the "freedom voices." On Capitol Hill, fifty of Fulbright's senatorial colleagues signed a joint resolution on behalf of RFE and RL at the bipartisan initiative of Democratic senator Hubert Humphrey and Republican Charles Percy. Before the fight was over, a total of seventy-seven senators had lent their names as cosponsors.

A key player in this effort was my old Munich colleague Ronny Ronalds. I have told how helpful to us Ronalds was from his post at VOA. In 1971, after five years with that outfit, he was due to be assigned to a senior foreign service post overseas with its parent organization, USIA. Instead, we persuaded him to return to Munich as director of RL, where there was a vacancy. While winding up his personal affairs in Washington, Ronalds worked with senators who supported RFE and RL, supplying them with factual material for speeches. He was instrumental in helping the staff of Senator Percy recruit other senators as cosponsors of the resolution aimed at saving the organizations.

Still, the impasse dragged on. With extinction drawing ever nearer, I took one more action. I had been tipped off that a faction at the *New York Times* was pressing for the paper to come out publicly in our behalf, but that resistance was coming from a key quarter: John Oakes, the editor of the editorial page. With that in mind, I picked up the telephone one Sunday afternoon and called Zbigniew Brzezinski at home. Brzezinski, then still a Columbia University professor, later became President Jimmy Carter's national security advisor; in those days his voice was already influential in foreign policy circles. I explained our plight and the need for haste. While we were talking, he devised a scheme to meet with another well-known academic, Hans Morgenthau. If Brzezinski had the reputation of a hawk, Morgenthau was equally known for his questioning of the Vietnam War. In that regard, they were poles apart.

Brzezinski persuaded Morgenthau to send with him a joint telegram to John Oakes at the *Times*. Later he read the text to me on the telephone. As I recall, it began like this: "We seldom agree on anything, but one thing on which we do agree is that Radio Free Europe and Radio Liberty should not be put quietly to death."

According to Brzezinski, Oakes clung to his opposition to RFE and RL but agreed that they should receive more of a public hearing before being terminated. He said he would publish an editorial on the subject.

Fortunately, the editorial was assigned to the leading Soviet expert on the editorial board, our friend Harry Schwartz. Harry exercised his mandate to the fullest, and the editorial became a ringing defense of RFE and RL. As if by magic, papers all over the country, many of which had up to now remained silent on the issue, followed the *Times's* lead.

Fulbright, facing public outrage and increasing isolation, finally acceded grudgingly to compromise legislation that kept RFE and RL alive for one more year. In August of the same year, 1972, President Nixon appointed a commission headed by Dr. Milton Eisenhower to look into a long-term solution. On the basis of the commission's recommendations, Congress passed the Board for International Broadcasting (BIB) Act, which created a new, overt funding mechanism for RFE and RL. The favorable vote in both houses of Congress was overwhelming, with Fulbright and two of his followers on the Foreign Relations Committee among the few dissenters.

So a powerful Washington figure was defeated. Even his own committee voted against him, for the first time since he had become chairman in 1959.

Why did Fulbright court this humiliation so stubbornly, in the face of what he knew to be massive resentment of his position, even by his old friends? We now know that RL and RFE were more than just a blip on the senator's radar screen, that they symbolized for him all that he had come to despise in U.S. foreign policy. In his book *The Crippled Giant: American Foreign Policy and Its Domestic Consequences*, written in summer 1972 just after his defeat on the issue, he devoted a major passage to RFE and RL in an early chapter, singling them out as leading "relics" of U.S. foreign policy "myopia." Here is some sample language:

> Purporting to keep the "truth" alive behind the "Iron Curtain," Radio Free Europe and Radio Liberty are in fact hardy survivors of the old cold-war mentality. If our foreign propaganda activities had anything at all to do with an authentic interest in freedom and truth rather than anti-communism, we would presumably be providing funds for a "Radio Free Greece" or a "Radio Free Brazil," both coun-

tries whose governments impose a degree of censorship. The rationale for Radio Free Europe and Radio Liberty, and for much of the official propaganda put forth by the United States Information Agency, derives from the old crusading anti-Communist ideology.[2]

Fulbright revealed his premise that such U.S. information activities were "wholly inconsistent with—and detrimental to—our emerging policy of accommodation with the Soviet Union." Fulbright was commonly believed to be bitter about the U.S. role in Vietnam and the Tonkin Gulf Resolution (which he had voted for) whose manipulation by the administration helped to escalate U.S. involvement. In his book, Fulbright showed that his resentment was now much deeper: he launched a retrospective attack on many earlier Cold War actions of the United States, which he had supported at the time, such as the "Truman Doctrine" aimed at keeping Greece and Turkey from the Soviet sphere of influence.[3]

In this same period the Soviet regime showed its appreciation of Fulbright's favorable political stance by bringing out in Russian translation his book-length 1967 critique of U.S. foreign policy, *Arrogance of Power*. For the Kremlin, this was an unusual gesture toward a living politician who could not be counted as firmly in the "socialist camp"; at the same time, the Soviets kept some distance from Fulbright by including an introduction to the Russian version *(Nadmennost' vlasti)* that was slightly mocking about the senator's class ties with the Arkansas landed gentry.

The Crippled Giant showed that Fulbright had been affected by the domestic political ferment of the 1960s. In the introduction he cited as an authority Herbert Marcuse, a guru of the New Left,[4] and in his conclusion trumpeted that "the dissenters of recent years have been sending their leaders a message, and there are signs that it is getting through."[5] Fulbright was referring, of course, to American dissenters; he wanted no truck with the Soviet variety.

Fulbright's public career was no stranger to contradiction and controversy. As a very junior Democratic senator, he had proposed after the Republicans won control of Congress in the 1946 elections that President Harry Truman name Republican senator Arthur Vandenberg as secretary of state and then resign; this would make Vandenberg, in the absence of a vice president, the Republican president of the United States. The suggestion led Truman to refer to Fulbright as Senator Halfbright, a name that was gleefully used in later years by Senator Joseph McCarthy and other political enemies.[6] On another occasion, Truman called Fulbright, a Rhodes Scholar and former university president, "an overeducated S.O.B."[7]

In his approach to policy Fulbright showed a strain of elitism that may help to explain his insensitivity to Soviet dissidents and their persecution at the hands of a government with which he sought accommodation. In his first senatorial campaign, in 1944, he declared: "I am not for Negro participation in our primary elections, and I do not approve of social equality."[8] In the Senate he routinely voted against civil rights legislation, even after some of his fellow southerners had had a change of heart.[9]

Well before the Vietnam War became the central issue of foreign policy, there were signs of Fulbright's growing alienation from the Establishment. It was reported that he was passed over for nomination as secretary of state by President John Kennedy because of his unacceptable record on civil rights.[10] President Johnson, who was piqued by Fulbright's flagging support of the Vietnam effort, professed to believe that this disappointment had come to be what really made Fulbright tick. "Fulbright's problem," LBJ claimed, "is that he's never found any president that would appoint him Secretary of State. . . . He wants the nation to stand up and take notice of Bill Fulbright, and he knows that the best way to get that attention is to put himself in the role of critic."[11]

By attacking RFE and RL, Fulbright got plenty of the attention Johnson thought he craved, but it cost him the respect of many who had supported him on other issues.[12]

August 1972, the month when the Eisenhower Commission was created, also marked my twentieth anniversary with RL. It had been troubling me for some time that I had never been able to set foot in the Soviet Union, the country that had been the focus of my entire professional activity. I decided that the time had come to move on to another job that would give me a chance to visit Moscow and other parts of the USSR. With RL's future now seemingly assured and its operations in Ronalds's capable hands in Munich, I felt free to leave. In September 1972 I joined the U.S. Information Agency in Washington as head of Soviet and East European research.

Although I did not know it, in many ways RL's Smuta, its Time of Troubles, was just beginning, and my own involvement with "Radio Hole-in-the-Head" was far from ended.

Notes

Elsewhere in this book source notes are not given, because the identity of the source, usually myself, should be clear. In trying to explain the virulence of Senator Fulbright's attacks on RFE and RL, however, I have consulted the senator's own writing and works by others.

1. Haynes Johnson and Bernard M. Gwertzman, *Fulbright: The Dissenter* (Garden City, N.Y.: Doubleday, 1968), p. 108.
2. J. William Fulbright, *The Crippled Giant: American Foreign Policy and Its Domestic Consequences* (New York: Random House, 1972), pp. 37–38.
3. Ibid. See especially chap. 1, "The Truman Doctrine in Europe and the World." Fulbright was also highly critical of George Kennan's famous 1947 article in *Foreign Affairs,* called the "X" article because of the pseudonym used by the author, whose theory of "containment" is generally credited as the underpinning of U.S. policy during the Cold War.
4. Ibid., p. 8.
5. Ibid., p. 279.
6. For one version of this, see David McCullough, *Truman* (New York: Simon and Schuster, 1992), p. 523.
7. Ibid., p. 864.
8. Johnson and Gwertzman, *Fulbright,* p. 83.
9. Fulbright was one of the signers in 1956 of the "Southern Manifesto" outlining opposition to the 1954 Supreme Court ruling on desegregation of schools. Lyndon Johnson did not sign.
10. See, for example, Clark Clifford, *Counsel to the President: A Memoir* (New York: Random House, 1991), p. 339.
11. Doris Kearns (now Doris Kearns Goodwin), *Lyndon Johnson and the American Dream* (New York: Harper & Row, 1976), p. 313.
12. In this chapter, I have told about the "Save the Radios" efforts from the perspective of events that I experienced personally. Much of the story here has never been told before in print. Obviously, many individuals and activities omitted from this narrative were also involved. For different angles, the reader is invited to consult other sources, such as Sig Mickelson, *America's Other Voice* (New York: Praeger, 1983), and Cord Meyer, *Facing Reality* (Washington, D.C.: University Press of America, 1982). Cord Meyer was a CIA official who for many years dealt with RFE and RL from behind the scenes.

Merger Traumas 13

The Board for International Broadcasting (BIB) Act of 1973 kept RFE and RL alive, but at the price of turmoil. The cause of the upheaval was their consolidation under a single corporate roof, RFE/RL, Inc. In the wake of that event, Munich became a broadcasting battleground.

Despite the merger, the two organizations retained their separate identities and language services. The staff of RL was moved into the RFE building, crowding the former sole occupant. In the corridors and the canteen, Poles and Czechs had to coexist uneasily with Russians and Tatars. The former were apt to view the latter not only as intruders on their turf but also as representatives of the power that had oppressed their homeland. Moreover, the economies realized by pooling administrative and support staffs led to personnel cuts. When an employee of one organization was cut, his or her job went to a person from the rival radio. The situation, logical in budget terms, was made-to-order to exacerbate existing tensions.

At the management level there was an ongoing dispute about how to divide the corporation's combined resources between the two sides. Partisans of RFE believed that its Eastern European listeners were more anti-Communist and better friends of the West than were RL's Soviet audiences and that therefore they deserved the lion's share of broadcast attention. Partisans of RL, on the other hand, argued that freedom from Communism in Eastern Europe would have to wait until the Soviet Union was softened up from inside and that therefore broadcasts to that country should have priority.

In the CIA days RFE, which had been founded before RL and enjoyed much more public awareness thanks to its advertising campaigns, had always wangled larger budgets than RL had been able to obtain. Broadcasting in only six languages, RFE received 50 percent more funding than did RL with its more than one dozen language services. RFE's preferred status had always rankled at RL. It meant, for example, that RFE could devote far more personnel and airtime to broadcasting to Bulgaria, a country of only 9 million people, than RL could give to broadcasts for Ukraine, a Soviet republic with a population of 50 million people.

In my office at USIA I was out of this troubled picture, but old friends in Munich kept me in touch. One such old friend was Ronny Ronalds, now back at RL as its director.

Not all the news from Ronalds was bad, by any means. RL was experiencing a talent windfall, thanks to the new Soviet policy of dealing with dissidents and other nonconformists by exiling them abroad. Ronalds was working hard to seize the opportunity by bringing the new arrivals into RL. People who had been famous back in the Soviet Union were now being heard regularly in the broadcasts, either as freelance contributors or regular members of the staff. Among them were such figures as Viktor Nekrasov, whose novel *In the Trenches of Stalingrad* was the classic Soviet literary work about World War II; Andrei Sinyavsky, the writer who had been imprisoned for smuggling his work abroad under the pseudonym Abram Tertz; the popular Moscow actor and balladeer Alexander Galich; and Anatolii Kuznetsov, whose book *Babii Yar* about the German execution of Jews in Kiev had caused him trouble with anti-Semites in the Soviet establishment. The most famous exile of all, Alexander Solzhenitsyn, said some complimentary things about RL when Ronalds met with him soon after his arrival in the West, but he then disappeared into seclusion and never took an active part in the broadcasts. Still, there were dozens who did. Keeping such people on the payroll required funds, of course, and Ronalds twisted the arms of top management to get the funding.

The conflict of interests between RFE and RL was so deep that probably any two directors would have been at loggerheads. It was bad luck that Ronalds's opposite number at RFE happened to be a dour Munich RFE veteran named Ralph Walter, a hardworking but humorless authoritarian who never troubled to conceal his contempt for "Radio Hole-in-the-Head" and its free and easy way of doing things. When I got to know Walter later on, he made it clear that the creatively pluralistic give-and-take on which RL was founded was to him little better than anarchy. Now it was the task of Ronalds, with his sunny disposition and laid-back style, to stand toe to toe with the saturnine Walter and slug it out over resources. No two people could have been more poorly suited to work together.

I apologize for the bureaucratic detail that follows, but without it the drama of coming events can hardly be appreciated.

To supervise the newly merged operation in Munich and try to maintain harmony between the two sides, the board of directors of RFE/RL, Inc., in Washington had hired out of retirement a former RL director, Walter K. (Ken) Scott. Scott was trusted by the board to settle fairly disputes between the two broadcasting organizations. A mild-mannered, gentlemanly individual whose twin passions were serving his country and playing golf, he had spent most of his career as a U.S. diplomat. He had once been assigned to Munich as U.S. consul-general, which had given him early familiarity with RFE and RL and their problems. Then in the latter's CIA period he had come out of retirement to serve briefly as RL's director. Now he was coaxed off the links a second time to preside over the administrative consolidation of the radios. In 1977, just when he was preparing for a third retirement, he died suddenly on a golf course south of Munich.

Another significant player on the Munich scene in those days was C. Rodney Smith, a retired army major-general who years earlier had been sent to Munich to try to settle a factional dispute involving RFE's Czechoslovak service. Smith's handling of the delicate matter had commanded such respect the he was drafted to stay on for a time as RFE director. Like Scott, he was a patriotic individual dedicated to the overall goal of both RFE and RL, who had no special-interest axe to grind. Now he was in Munich for a second time, as a consultant to the newly formed Board for International Broadcasting.

Back home in Washington, there was still another player. Congress had set up the bipartisan BIB as the small government agency that would replace the CIA as the link between RFE/RL and federal funding. Its members were appointed by the president, subject to confirmation by the Senate, but once in office for a three-year term they were expected to act independently for the good of the organization.

In addition to channeling appropriations to RFE/RL, the BIB was entrusted with oversight over their activities. The oversight mandate was extremely vague; according to the BIB Act, the new agency was held responsible for ensuring that the broadcasts were "not inconsistent with the broad outlines of U.S. foreign policy." To perform its mission, the BIB was authorized to employ a staff.

The uncertainty surrounding the BIB mandate led to wildly varying interpretations of the new agency's role. Some of its staff, for example, saw themselves as actual managers of RFE/RL. On the other hand, members of the newly consolidated private board of directors of RFE/RL and some of their employees regarded the BIB and its staff as busybodies intent only on tampering with an effective operation.

In this new situation, there were old hands in Munich who would sigh wistfully for the relatively untroubled days of CIA involvement. The first period of life under the BIB was dominated by internecine feuding between it and the private board of RFE/RL, Inc., whose members were self-selected under the corporate charter. The private board had been retained as a guarantor of professional independence; now, despite its total reliance on federal funding, it seemed to see itself as answerable to no one. In this bureaucratic battle, issues were secondary, and it became a classic Washington struggle for turf. The warfare died down only years later when Congress, exasperated by the squabbling, amended the BIB Act to merge the two boards. In the meantime, the operation suffered, although—thanks once again to the dedication of the émigré staffs—the broadcasting never ceased.

In Munich some of Ronalds's arguments about giving RL a more equitable share of resources began to sink in with Ken Scott and others, including the new U.S.-based president of the combined corporation, Sig Mickelson, a former head of CBS News. Ronalds told me that he found support even from General Smith, despite the latter's close connection with RFE. Ralph Walter's reaction to these developments was, to say the least, unhappy, and his relations with Ronalds became increasingly abrasive. This was apparently the reason why he was soon relieved of his executive authority and transferred back to the Washington office in virtual limbo.

Meanwhile, my own life was touched by the BIB's appointment of a man named Walter Roberts as its executive director. Roberts was a jovial Viennese refugee who had successfully scaled the American bureaucratic ladder. He had been associate director of USIA, the person who in 1972 was responsible for having that agency hire me. In the process we became friends. Now that he had come out of retirement to work for the BIB, he began to urge me to join him there.

I was enjoying my work at USIA, which in four years had taken me three times to the Soviet Union and at least once to every country of Eastern Europe (except Albania). At the same time, I was aware that relations between the BIB and the Munich staffs of RFE/RL had soured, and I thought that my RL experience and my good relations with Walter Roberts might help me smooth things over. Another factor in my decision was that the BIB's program officer was Anatole (Tony) Shub, son of David and younger brother of Boris Shub. After a career with the *Washington Post,* at one point as head of its Moscow bureau, Tony (called Tolya by his family and Russian friends) had gravitated to the BIB via RFE's Munich newsroom, which he had headed for a time. Finally, after much soul-searching (and arm-twisting by Roberts and Shub), I made the move in September 1976, becoming the BIB's planning and research officer.

In November 1976, two months after I joined the BIB staff, Jimmy Carter was elected president. As a lifelong Democrat, I was pleased. When Carter announced that he was appointing Zbigniew Brzezinski, a former Polish refugee, as head of the National Security Council (NSC), I was aware that Brzezinski had detractors as well as admirers among his academic colleagues, but my happy memory of his effort to help save RFE/RL by using his influence with the *New York Times* made me optimistic. Carter also announced the designation of John Gronouski, a former postmaster-general and ambassador to Poland under President Johnson, as chairman of the BIB.

On Capitol Hill there were mutterings that Gronouski was a "has-been." There were also indications that Brzezinski had not been fully involved in his appointment, which had heavy domestic-political overtones, given Gronouski's involvement with the Polish-American community. (In fact, Gronouski spoke hardly a word of Polish; his mother's maiden name was Riley.) The story that Gronouski had once been arrested for driving while intoxicated spread quickly in Washington. Then our new chairman shot himself in the foot by loudly proclaiming that he wanted RFE/RL to offer the Soviet Union and the Eastern European Communist countries the "right of reply" to any RFE/RL broadcasts they felt were inaccurate. Gronouski's intention was to maneuver the Communist bloc into accepting the role of RFE/RL as legitimate, but given the political realities of the day it aroused a storm of criticism from both right and left at the idea of the U.S. Congress funding a Communist "right of reply." During his term as chairman, Gronouski, a decent man, never recovered from the self-inflicted wound.

In the midst of all this, I had a telephone call from a person named Paul B. Henze, whom I had known years earlier in Munich when he was assigned to the staff of RFE. Our wives had had babies at the same time in the same German clinic, a powerful bonding experience for two American women in those unfamiliar surroundings. Now Henze informed me proudly that he had been called back from an assignment in Turkey to work under Brzezinski at the White House NSC, where RFE/RL would be one of his major responsibilities. He came over to the house for dinner a few times and made it clear that he did not intend to sit quietly on the sidelines. He referred affectionately to his old friend Ralph Walter, with whom he had stayed in close touch since their college days at St. Olaf's, a Lutheran institution founded to celebrate "the Nordic Middle Ages" and ever since devoted to education "rooted in the Christian Gospel." Reclining now in one of our armchairs, Henze said things about the BIB staff on which I was serving that seemed to me decidedly un-Christian. I was impressed with the depth of his disdain for any and all with whom he disagreed.

I must acknowledge that during his time at the NSC, Henze lobbied hard to increase federal support for RFE/RL. In this he was helped by the tension created by the 1979 Soviet invasion of Afghanistan and the 1981 bombing of the RFE/RL building in Munich, which led immediately to suspicion that it was the work of Soviet or East European agents.

At the same time, my colleagues on the BIB staff registered dismay over Henze's meddling with the internal workings of RFE/RL. He began immediately to deal directly with the chairman of the private board, a veteran of commercial broadcasting named John Hayes. In doing so, he circumvented the BIB, which by legislative intent was meant to be the nexus for government relations with RFE/RL. It was ironic that after all the effort expended by so many people to create the BIB as a means of getting RFE/RL out from under the CIA, the broadcasters were now taking direction from a man described by the *New York Times* as "a former CIA station chief in Turkey" and identified elsewhere in the public prints as a CIA employee from the time of his assignment to RFE in the 1950s. I have no knowledge that in his later dealings with RFE/RL Henze was pursuing the CIA's agenda and not his own, but his own was bad enough.

During his career, Henze has been no stranger to controversy. While he was at the NSC, Representative Elizabeth Holtzman called on President Carter to dismiss him for a remark he made defending RFE's broadcast of an interview with Bishop Valerian Trifa, a Romanian war criminal who was stripped of his U.S. citizenship and deported. Later on, after the attempted assassination of Pope John

Paul II in 1982, when Henze was no longer in office, he became an ardent proponent of the theory that there was a "Bulgarian connection," although in time an Italian court failed to convict the Bulgarians charged with complicity in the attempt. That same year he wrote a vitriolic letter to the *New York Times* attacking five American academics who had criticized human rights abuses in Turkey.

Gronouski's political weakness played into Henze's hands. In short order, with the acquiescence of RFE/RL board chairman John Hayes, Henze's friend Ralph Walter had been reassigned to Munich, this time as vice president for policy and programs. That made Walter the lord of RL as well as RFE, and he thereby became Ronalds's boss. In that top job, Walter showed signs of low regard for the old RL executive staff. RL veterans began to complain that they were feeling Walter's dislike in a variety of ways. Max Ralis, for example, was forced to retire earlier than he had planned.

In this situation, Ronalds had scant chance of defending RL's interests effectively. This left him little choice but to give up the directorship of RL and return to the United States. For personal reasons, after a total of nineteen years in Munich, he and his wife were happy to go home. In time he rejoined VOA. Over the years Ronalds had done more than any other American to build RL into the effective instrument that it had become. He had an instinctive sense of leadership, of what was right for a Russian audience and how to put together and nurture the teams that could provide it. Now, the new people at the levers of command were unaware of—or indifferent to—his outstanding contribution, and he left Munich with little fanfare. With Ralph Walter in power, even old friends and admirers were afraid to speak publicly about their feelings for Ronalds, for fear of compromising their own jobs.

It says something about Ralph Walter's attitude toward RL that he simply left its directorship open, apparently thinking that he could run it with his left hand. It was another five years before RL had a new director.

This neglect had to be reflected, sooner or later, in the quality of the broadcasts. Eventually, it was Walter's undoing, but only after more years of Smuta for RL and its staff.

Given the Henze-Hayes-Walter axis and its contemptuous circumvention of the BIB, our work on the staff degenerated into a kind of meaningless routine. Tony Shub and I tried to keep busy by evaluating the broadcasts, a statutory function of the BIB that its adversaries were powerless to prevent. Since I was one of a handful of Americans who knew the Uzbek language, I focused on the output of that service, while also trying to keep an eye on other languages where there might be problems.

For the other services, we hired distinguished outside specialists with the requisite linguistic and area knowledge, usually from the academic world. Some of the evaluations were outstanding documents that pinpointed significant shortcomings in the programs, but because they bore the stamp of the odious BIB they received little attention or follow-up from Ralph Walter and his staff in Munich.

Otherwise, I was involved in few tasks during that period that gave me any sense of real achievement. An exception—one project that I do recall with considerable satisfaction—involved audience research. As the BIB's planning and research officer, I was directly responsible for oversight of audience research. At one point, that activity was mortally threatened.

Sig Mickelson's successor as president of RFE/RL, appointed by the private board of directors chaired by John Hayes, was a man whose chief credential seemed to consist of having made a lot of money in commercial broadcasting. Since I can think of no way to praise him, I prefer to let him be nameless here. One of his most memorable actions was to bring into the operation an old friend named "Dud" (whose real name I omit here for the same reason). To find employment for his friend, he created a new executive position that made Dud boss over both Max Ralis, head of RL's audience research, and Henry Hart, Ralis's opposite number at RFE. Dud's only claim to be audience research czar of RFE/RL seemed to be that he had knocked around FM stations in the United States.

Dud and his boss, undaunted by their lack of familiarity with the geographic area or the intricate cross-cultural methodology that had been devised by Ralis at RL and used with equally good results by Hart at RFE, set about to discredit their work—for reasons that one can only guess at. Reports began to circulate that the audience research at both stations was seriously flawed. There were even suggestions that Ralis and Hart were systematically faking the data. Admittedly, the sampling techniques on which RFE/RL's audience research was based are always vulnerable to derision by the uninitiated, since from the outside they look like smoke and mirrors. Nevertheless, people in business have grown rich using the same basic techniques.

When these scandalous reports about RFE/RL audience research reached the BIB, they caused consternation. Listenership estimates were the backbone of our annual budget requests to the executive branch and Congress. If the research was phony, that undermined the whole operation. The private board of RFE/RL was equally taken aback by the developments, even though it had put in place the men who were causing them.

Chairman Gronouski and Executive Director Roberts, with low-key support from the RFE/RL board, assigned me to conduct an investigation of audience research. Although I knew the principals involved–some of whom, like Max Ralis and his deputy Gene Parta, were my good friends–I resolved as a matter of professional conscience to let the chips fall where they might.

In my years at USIA I had had quite a bit of exposure to survey research techniques, which rely on statistical sampling, something that I had studied at MIT. I began the investigation by visiting interview sites in Copenhagen (RL) and Vienna (RFE). There I talked at length with interviewers and scrutinized page after page of the raw data that in "weighted" form were used to generate listenership estimates. With help from experts at USIA and at MIT, I reviewed everything from data collection to the weighting process, which in the case of RL involved the computer simulation I have referred to in an earlier chapter. Leo Bogart, a past president of the American Association for Public Opinion Research (and also of the World Association of Public Opinion Research), was generous in volunteering assistance.

To my relief, everything checked out. I wrote a report that, barring a few minor criticisms, gave audience research at both RFE and RL a clean bill of health. Dud's wings were clipped, and in time he and his boss disappeared from the scene, without having questioned my report with any degree of credibility. Normalcy was restored to the audience research operations. Gronouski and Roberts thanked me for defending a valuable American asset, but if the private RFE/RL board felt any gratitude toward me for saving its corporate bacon it kept its feelings to itself.

Another activity that helped to make life worthwhile during this dreary period was my participation as BIB representative in an inter-agency Nationalities Working Group that brought together the State Department, CIA, National Security Agency, Pentagon, and other elements of the government for the purpose of overcoming decades of neglect of the non-Russian peoples and territories of the Soviet Union.

Ironically, this group was chaired by Paul Henze on behalf of the NSC. When it came to the nationalities question, Paul and I were able to set aside our differences and work together. In particular, I helped him with information about Central Asia, an area of which he knew little.

But on matters involving the BIB and RFE/RL, I had no doubt that Henze saw me as an enemy. He confirmed this later on: before leaving office at the end of the Carter administration, he wrote a letter to John Hayes on White House stationery condemning the entire BIB staff, without exception, in bitter terms. Hayes, who liked to stir things up, puckishly sent a copy to Walter Roberts.

Given the strained relations between the BIB and the NSC, it is amusing that during this period a Soviet newspaper published a report that I (not Henze) was Brzezinski's right-hand man for RFE/RL and that Brzezinski had instructed me to prepare for him a "confidential memorandum" to be sent to Munich as his ukase. Since Soviet intelligence must have known that the true state of affairs was exactly the opposite—it was no secret in Washington—I assumed that Moscow was just having a little fun at our expense.

As for the Nationalities Working Group, unfortunately its labor under Henze's chairmanship resulted mainly in bureaucratic paper pushing. Henze had a preachy, "do it or else" style that irritated senior officials. Although he continually invoked the authority of the White House, where our meetings were held, he was no match for the wiles of crafty Washington bureaucrats. Some confided in me their belief that he was more talk than action. Still, the group's existence did help to heighten awareness in Washington of the non-Russian Soviet republics. Some of its momentum carried over into the Reagan administration when it continued to meet, but less and less frequently. Finally, it quietly expired. Whether or not Henze missed an opportunity for leadership, successive U.S. administrations seemed determined to ignore the political trends that were already leading to the breakup of the Soviet Union.

Before the Carter administration ended, with Henze still in the White House, I was caught up in an episode that marked the crescendo of my lifelong involvement with Radio Liberty and, ultimately, its coda.

One for the
Good Guys

14

Predictably, problems arose from the RL leadership vacuum caused by Ralph Walter's disdainful failure to replace Ronalds with another director. By 1980, three years after Ronalds's departure and toward the end of President Carter's term, the problems had begun to surface ever more insistently.

Like most other media organizations, RFE/RL had internal guidelines. In the early days of the merger, a new combined set of guidelines had been worked out in concert with the BIB. Among other things, they helped to reassure members of Congress that if they voted funds for RFE/RL, things would not go haywire. The guidelines were broadly permissive, as in this example: "The essence of RFE/RL's program policy continues to be the practice of independent, professionally competent, and responsible broadcast journalism." At the same time, there were some commonsense caveats:

- "RFE and RL are . . . committed to respect for human rights and the principles of democracy."
- "They are nonsectarian, defending freedom of religious faith and observance for all creeds."
- "Historical events should be approached in a critical as well as a tolerant spirit, avoiding chauvinistic or sectarian bias."
- "RFE and RL programs express respect for all peoples, religions, and cultures and should under no circumstances fan or fuel chauvinism."

To prevent violation of the guidelines, radio management in Munich employed a special staff of analysts who reviewed the programs daily and issued summary reports. The reports were shared with us at the BIB. Of course, the reports were effective only when they reflected the actual content of the broadcasts.

We on the BIB staff also relied on making our own evaluations from time to time, as mentioned in the last chapter. To get the programs, we had to make a formal request to Munich for a sample of the output, usually a week's worth in a given language. In Munich, RFE/RL management complied with our requests, if only grudgingly, because–given our oversight mandate from Congress–it had no choice. But if we asked informally for a copy of this or that broadcast that was not in an official sample, there was usually foot-dragging. We wondered whether the Munich managers thought they had a shield in the Carter White House that gave them license to thumb their noses at the BIB. Their manner suggested strongly that they did.

Pretty soon, evidence began to pile up that in RL's Russian broadcasts violations were occurring with alarming frequency. Concerned employees began calling me surreptitiously at their own expense from their home phones in Munich. Bootleg copies of certain broadcast scripts began to show up in my mailbox at home, German postage stamps on the envelopes.

The main problem seemed to center on historical broadcasts edited by a certain Russian nationalist. It was particularly disquieting to find, when I compared the scripts with the daily broadcast summaries, that the latter had glossed over the violations.

One of the scripts that I found in my mailbox was dedicated to Konstantin Pobedonostsev, a turn-of-the-century political and religious figure whose name to Russians is synonymous with all that was reactionary in the late tsarist period. The American historian Richard Pipes has called Pobedonostsev, who was associated with the notorious Black Hundreds, the "Grand Inquisitor" of a movement that was "steadily more xenophobic and anti-Semitic." Now RL was praising Pobedonostsev as a "great conservative thinker," the title of its program devoted to him. Further programs were similarly laudatory about other known anti-Semites. There was a tendency in the broadcasts to belittle democracy and non-Russian peoples. One program even attacked the long-suffering Ukrainian Catholic Church, which had been savagely suppressed by Stalin and driven underground as its churches and other property were taken away from it by the official Russian Orthodox hierarchy in Moscow.

As I read these scripts I thought of good Russians like Academician Andrei Sakharov, of other democratic dissidents who were then risking their lives and their freedom to struggle for the humanitarian principles that RL was now attacking. I was in touch with Andrei Sinyavsky and others who had taken refuge in the West after undergoing KGB harassment and persecution, some of whom had spent years in the gulag for their beliefs; such people told me of their dismay at what RL was doing to betray their democratic cause. I remembered Boris Shub, the spiritual father of RL, stamping around our building at Oberwiesenfeld in the early days as he fulminated against ethnic and religious intolerance. I pictured scores of others who had worked hard over the decades to establish RL's reputation as a beacon of democratic values. I thought of the U.S. taxpayer footing the bill for Soviet audiences to hear garbage that was the antithesis of everything truly American.

Others at the BIB shared my concern but when we complained to the current RFE/RL management the response invariably consisted of the same dual argument: that the violations in question were only a small part of the total broadcast output and that most of the broadcasts were unexceptionable, some of them indeed very good. Glenn Ferguson, then president of RFE/RL, and Ralph Walter, his vice president for programs whose problems with RL were described in the last chapter, were telling us, in effect, that Radio Liberty was only a little bit pregnant. When our board rather halfheartedly pressed them for action it received only vague assurances, no specific commitments. Meanwhile, unforgivable and damaging programs continued to go on the air.

To break the logjam in the face of Ralph Walter's lack of cooperation, I devised a go-for-broke plan. With the blessings of Chairman Gronouski and Executive Director Roberts, I flew quietly to Munich without informing the RFE/RL staff. In my suitcase were a shortwave receiver and recording equipment. At Munich Airport on a cold January day, I picked up a rental car and drove south on the icy Autobahn, turning off to a minuscule Bavarian village called Grosshartpenninck that happened to be only a few kilometers from the RFE/RL transmitter base at Holzkirchen. There I holed up in a primitive rural inn and set up the equipment in my room. For nearly a week, with perfect reception from the transmitters right down the road, I taped RL broadcasts in Russian and other languages. There was time out only for hurried, unappetizing meals in the *Kneipe* downstairs, a few hours of sleep between tapings, and the single luxury of stretching my legs once each afternoon by trudging through the snow to the even tinier village of Kleinhartpenninck just over a hill. At the end of my stint in Grosshartpenninck I hurried back to Washington with a shopping bag full of cassette recordings.

The off-air recordings documented a breakdown of management control that was even worse than we had expected. Not only were there more policy violations, there were other anomalies as well. The transmitters, for example, would suddenly switch languages in the middle of a program: a listener tuned in to a scheduled Tatar program might find it replaced in mid-sentence by one in Estonian. KGB sabotage or simple negligence? It was impossible to tell.

Back in Washington, Walter Roberts gave me only three days to write up my findings in time for a scheduled meeting of the BIB members. By now Reagan had just replaced Carter as president, Paul Henze was out of the White House, and a Republican member of the board, a Washington lawyer named Charles Ablard who had learned his way around the bureaucracy from a former post as counsel of the Army Department, was named acting chairman—standard procedure when a change in administration involves a change in parties. I was to find Ablard, an old friend of Walter Roberts, as generally supportive of my efforts as former chairman Gronouski, now a rank-and-file Democratic member of the board.

We knew that my report could be damaging to everyone at RFE/RL, not just the culprits, if it fell into the hands of ill-wishers who might try to sensationalize it out of proportion. For that reason, I kept the text within the four walls of the BIB. Just enough copies were made for each member to have one at the board meeting held on our premises.

I also knew, in view of the history of bad feeling between the BIB and radio management, that skeptics would suspect me of deliberately inflating the problem. In writing the report, I took pains to document every criticism with specifics.

At the BIB meeting, after having copies of the report placed in front of each member, Chairman Ablard asked me to give an oral summary of the highlights. I began by noting that everything I had to say was backed by tapes and scripts. As I went on to describe elements of RL's Russian broadcasts that were antidemocratic, anti-Western, anti-Polish, anti-Catholic, and even anti-Semitic, I could see that I had the attention of my audience. At the end, the board adopted a formal resolution instructing RFE/RL president Glenn Ferguson, who regularly attended its meetings as an ex officio member, to take action without delay to eliminate the abuses and report back to it. Then members of the board, noting the potentially incendiary repercussions of my report if made public, requested anxiously that the copies of it be gathered up and placed under lock and key. A staff member did so.

We had achieved the hoped-for result. RL's Russian historical series underwent a transformation. Although there were still occasional problems, they were minor compared with the egregious breaches that had occurred before my report pinpointed them.

My personal satisfaction at this outcome was soon tarnished, however. Within days of the BIB meeting, the *Washington Post* and other newspapers around the country carried an article by syndicated columnist Jack Anderson that quoted from my report and identified me by name. For a civil servant, nothing can be worse than to appear in a Jack Anderson column, especially if it praises him. Such was Anderson's reputation around Washington. Moreover, there is a tendency to believe that many people leak their own documents because they find no other way to draw attention to a problem. An old friend at the State Department cautioned me with a wry grin: "Jim, everybody's going to think you did it yourself."

As it turned out, he was probably right. Apparently, few people stopped to reason that, having achieved the purpose, I could only taint my own cause by leaking the report. As for the true identity of the leaker, I have no proof but deep down am sure I know who it was, a colleague who could only have been acting from professional jealousy (one whose name appears nowhere in this narrative).

Still, success was tangible. Shortly after the Anderson column appeared, a tough little Russian woman showed up in my office. I had heard of Ludmilla Alexeyeva, a legendary figure who had repeatedly defied the KGB as head of the Moscow Helsinki Watch Committee before the regime finally sent her to the West to get rid of her. Alexeyeva cheered me up by praising my report extravagantly. Then she startled me by telling me that she and her associates were going to publish excerpts in the English-language magazine *Russia,* which was being edited in the United States by another well-known ex-dissident, Valerii Chalidze. Another leak!

"How on earth did you get the report?" I asked Alexeyeva.

"Listen, dear boy," she told me, "if the KGB can't keep secrets from us, what makes you think you American bureaucrats can?"

Substantial portions of the report duly appeared in *Russia.* This time I didn't mind the leak so much. For one thing, that particular issue had a portrait of Sakharov on the cover. These were the good guys. I had a mental image of those French patriots in the film *Casablanca* drowning out the Nazi officers with their singing of the "Marseillaise."

For years afterwards reverberations from the report kept coming back to me. Soon after I wrote it, a version of it had reached Alexander Solzhenitsyn in his Vermont retreat. I knew this because rumblings of the Nobel Prize winner's discontent soon appeared in the Russian émigré press. Fourteen years later, following his return to Russia, Solzhenitsyn was still fulminating about what I had done. Someone sent me the tape of his talk show aired March 13, 1995, on Russian national television, in which he claimed that "the famous *[sic]* Critchlow expedition" was "extraordinarily biased, ignorant and incompetent, but with a definite aim." My aim, Solzhenitsyn said, waving his arms angrily, was to introduce "censorship" of RL broadcasts. He said at the time he had written a letter of complaint to President Reagan. Now, in 1995, Solzhenitsyn averred that RL should be shut down because of what "Critchlow's advice" had done to it.

Some of the concrete things that Solzhenitsyn said about the report have convinced me that he was misinformed about it. For example, he claimed that I had prevented RL from commemorating the six-hundredth anniversary of the Battle of Kulikovo Pole, which marked an important Russian victory over the Tatars. If he had seen an accurate version of the report, he should have understood that all my comments about the broadcasts, far from being "censorship," were made after they had already gone on the air. In the case of the victory over the Tatars, I had merely regretted the broadcast's tone of ethnic hatred and its possible impact on relations with the 6 million Tatars currently living in the Soviet Union, concluding: "Given that for centuries now Russians and Tatars have lived side by side in peace, could not RL have sounded a note of conciliation?"

As to my own attitude toward Solzhenitsyn, I have never ceased to admire him for his example of personal courage, but his political judgment is another matter.

Some months into the Reagan administration, a man named Frank Shakespeare was appointed chairman of the BIB. Shakespeare's first action, which he took immediately on being sworn in, was to fire both Glenn Ferguson and Ralph Walter, ordering them to vacate their offices at once. I had no advance knowledge of this action, which Shakespeare never discussed with me, but in the light of what had been happening in Munich it was difficult for me to quarrel with it.

Shakespeare, a very ideological right-wing Republican, created new turmoil at the Radios. He replaced Glenn Ferguson and Ralph Walter with people who seemed to be chosen more for their political views than for any broadcasting credentials. I had to flag a new outbreak of policy violations, this time in the Ukrainian service, and also involving anti-Semitic overtones. In time, action was taken to eliminate the problems. And in time, as Shakespeare's antics began to cause raised eyebrows in the White House and the State Department, he left the scene to become ambassador to Portugal, where he was surrounded by a competent professional staff of foreign service officers. He was replaced at the BIB by a moderate Republican, Malcolm Forbes, Jr., of *Forbes* magazine, whom I credit with ending antidemocratic biases and infusing RFE/RL with a new professionalism. Forbes's influence stood RFE/RL in good stead as the Communist regimes in the Soviet Union and Eastern Europe entered their death agonies. He served until the incoming administration of President Bill Clinton, according to custom, replaced him with a Democrat, former representative Dan Mica. By then my involvement with the BIB had ended.

Congressional action in combining the BIB and the private corporate board of RFE/RL, enjoining that both boards have the same membership, ended the feuding between them. How could they feud with themselves? But now that the chairman of the BIB, our boss, was also chairman of RFE/RL, Inc., he understandably tended to work directly through the RFE/RL staff and to bypass us. I stayed on at the BIB for a few more lackluster years but found it increasingly difficult to justify my generous federal salary. There was also the continuing unpleasantness of having people who knew me mostly through the Jack Anderson leak look at me as if I were the skunk at the picnic. In their eyes I was that dread Washington monster, the whistle-blower.

In 1985 I left government for academe, embarking on a happy and rewarding new life, but with decidedly no regrets about the part of my old one that had been dedicated to "Radio Hole-in-the-Head." I was proud to have been present at the creation of a Radio Liberty that grew from shaky, strife-torn beginnings to become a potent force for positive change in Soviet society. Today I still rejoice at the often strange but magnificent people with whom those years brought me into contact, enriching my life beyond all measure.

This book has been an attempt to portray RL from the inside. Gauging its effectiveness is more properly left to outsiders. Perhaps someday historians and social scientists will be able to detail the extent of RL's role in stimulating the pressures that led to perestroika and the eventual collapse of the system. Let me just note here that even after Gorbachev's experiments with glasnost opened the floodgates to a variety of information sources, RL broadcasts remained important. In his book *Dismantling Utopia: How Information Ended the Soviet Union,* Scott Shane, who was in Moscow as *Baltimore Sun* correspondent, described RL's role in keeping citizens informed of events during the August 1991 coup, when it looked for days as if the Old Guard of the Communist Party would be able to reassert control. For further evidence, just do as I often have done and ask any of RL's devoted listeners. They will tell you that Radio Liberty and the ideas it brought to its audiences were a potent influence for change in the Soviet world.

Epilogue: End of the Cold War

Radio Liberty's growth and development were the combined result of many people's labor and inspiration. All those who worked there in the early days are gone from the scene now. Many are no longer living. I have already described the tragedy that ended Boris Shub's life. His father David continued writing radio scripts until only a few months before his own death at eighty-four. Howland Sargeant played his usual lunchtime game of squash one day at the age of seventy-two, then returned home for a nap from which he never awoke. Victor Frank was felled by a stroke while dining in his beloved haven, London's Reform Club. When I arrived in Munich for a visit in spring 1992, I asked about Pylayev and was told he had died just the week before, well into his seventies. My wife Pat, who stayed with me through good times and bad, died from breast cancer at much too early an age, living just long enough to hold in her arms her newborn granddaughter Alanna. Others who stayed with RL or, like me, went on to second careers are now for the most part retired or semi-retired. A few—one of them Ronny Ronalds at VOA—are still in harness. Ronny and I happened to cross paths in Moscow in the final days of the Soviet regime, in September 1991, thirty-eight years after we had first met in Munich to try to start a radio station. The *St. Louis Post-Dispatch* ran a picture of us standing arm in arm in front of the Uzbekistan Restaurant after a convivial lunch—two grizzled "veterans of the Cold War" (in the words of the caption) looking, I'm afraid, rather pleased with ourselves and a lot older than we had in that far-off Munich time.

Somehow in those early days at Radio Liberty we managed to forge an organization that unlocked people's creative energies, that enabled them to bring to the airwaves a vitality and spontaneity that inspired listeners in faraway places. I have often reflected, since leaving, on the difference between the heady atmosphere of those days and the grinding, stultifying monotony of other bureaucracies. The single most important ingredient in our success, I have concluded, was the extraordinary individuals who worked there—not just because of their exceptional talent, but also because of their belief in the fundamental values of democracy, a belief that made them willing to stand up to the Kremlin and to institutional tyrants closer to home.

In this book I have tried to tell the story of those people. I am grateful to them for helping me learn many things: about other societies, their history and politics, and about how to work with people from diverse ethnic and cultural backgrounds in a spirit of personal and national humility. My twenty years with Radio Liberty were the experience of a lifetime.

At RL in the old days we used to joke that we were trying to work ourselves out of a job. Now that the Cold War is over, that may happen to those who are still there. Although international broadcasting is cheap compared to military and other security outlays, recent drastic budget cuts were inevitable, given the U.S. deficit and the reported profligacy of top management in paying itself outrageously high salaries. Yet I was glad to see the Clinton administration modify its original intention of closing down Radio Liberty and Radio Free Europe, in favor of keeping them alive in at least truncated form, from new headquarters in a palace in Prague.

What is important is to preserve the basic core of RFE/RL against future needs. There is a danger that RFE and RL will lose their special identities under the new structure devised by the Clinton administration and both parties on Capitol Hill, one that places all U.S. overseas broadcasting under the same board of governors. If RFE and RL are ever needed again in the old way, if a new authoritarian regime emerges to replace Soviet power, it may be too late to resurrect them from burial in the federal bureaucracy. Worst of all, the management of this critical national asset has been told that all federal funding will be ended by 1999.

Also of importance are technical facilities. If transmitters are dismantled instead of being mothballed, it will take five years to procure new ones and get them operating, too long to rise to a sudden political threat.

The record of Radio Liberty shows that millions of Russians and other peoples of the former Soviet empire responded to an outside voice that spoke to them not as a representative of a foreign government, but as a bearer of universal values expressed in terms of their own unique heritage and special problems. With the final victory of democracy in the republics of the former Soviet Union still very much in doubt, it is too early to discard the concept that made Radio Liberty a success. I hope that this book will help to keep it alive.

Index